Rugby in Global Perspective

This book critically examines how rugby union has developed in recent years, in nations on the periphery of the sport. Focusing on people and places on the fringes, it examines contemporary issues and challenges within the global game.

Such a collection is timely, as the sport's governing body seeks to expand influence and participation beyond the eight core nations, with the 2019 Rugby World Cup in Japan being the first time that that tournament has taken place outside of the core. Presenting case studies from Europe, Africa, North and South America, Asia and the Middle East, this collection offers an interdisciplinary account of a sport that is undergoing a period of significant change. Through examination of topics such as the development of rugby sevens and the growth of women's rugby, it considers what the future may hold for the sport.

Rugby in Global Perspective is important reading for students of sport in society, the globalisation of sport, sports studies, sport development and associated fields. It is also a valuable resource for academic researchers working in rugby union or sport in the peripheral rugby nations, as well as those with an interest in cultural geography, sociology, development studies, events studies, event management and sport management.

John Harris is Associate Dean Research in the Glasgow School for Business and Society at Glasgow Caledonian University, UK.

Nicholas Wise is a Senior Lecturer in Tourism and Event Management at Liverpool John Moores University, UK.

Routledge Focus on Sport, Culture and Society

Routledge Focus on Sport, Culture and Society showcases the latest cutting-edge research in the sociology of sport and exercise. Concise in form (20,000–50,000 words) and published quickly (within three months), the books in this series represents an important channel through which authors can disseminate their research swiftly and make an impact on current debates. We welcome submissions on any topic within the socio-cultural study of sport and exercise, including but not limited to subjects such as gender, race, sexuality, disability, politics, the media, social theory, Olympic Studies and the ethics and philosophy of sport. The series aims to be theoretically informed, empirically grounded and international in reach and will include a diversity of methodological approaches.

Available in this series:

5 **Rethinking Sports and Integration**
   Developing a Transnational Perspective on Migrants and Descendants in Sports
   Sine Agergaard

6 **Sport, Education and Corporatisation**
   Spaces of Connection, Contestation and Creativity
   Geoffery Z. Kohe and Holly Collison

7 **Who Owns Sport?**
   Edited by Andrew Adams and Leigh Robinson

8 **Rugby in Global Perspective**
   Playing on the Periphery
   Edited by John Harris and Nicholas Wise

https://www.routledge.com/sport/series/RFSCS

Rugby in Global Perspective
Playing on the Periphery

Edited by John Harris and Nicholas Wise

LONDON AND NEW YORK

First published 2020 by Routledge

2 Park Square, Milton Park, Abingdon, Oxon, OX14 4RN
605 Third Avenue, New York, NY 10017

Routledge is an imprint of the Taylor & Francis Group, an informa business

First issued in paperback 2020

Copyright © 2020 selection and editorial matter, John Harris and Nicholas Wise; individual chapters, the contributors

The right of John Harris and Nicholas Wise to be identified as the authors of the editorial material, and of the authors for their individual chapters, has been asserted in accordance with sections 77 and 78 of the Copyright, Designs and Patents Act 1988.

All rights reserved. No part of this book may be reprinted or reproduced or utilised in any form or by any electronic, mechanical, or other means, now known or hereafter invented, including photocopying and recording, or in any information storage or retrieval system, without permission in writing from the publishers.

Notice:
Product or corporate names may be trademarks or registered trademarks, and are used only for identification and explanation without intent to infringe.

British Library Cataloguing-in-Publication Data
A catalogue record for this book is available from the British Library

Library of Congress Cataloging-in-Publication Data
A catalog record has been requested for this book

ISBN: 978-0-367-33539-7 (hbk)
ISBN: 978-0-367-78783-7 (pbk)

Typeset in Times New Roman
by codeMantra

Contents

List of figures vii
List of tables viii
List of contributors ix
Acknowledgements xi

1 **Japan 2019 and the internationalisation of rugby union** 1
JOHN HARRIS AND NICHOLAS WISE

2 **Challenging the core: the rise of Argentina in international rugby** 12
NICHOLAS WISE AND JOHN HARRIS

3 **Against all odds: Fijiana's flight from zero to hero in the Rugby World Cup** 24
YOKO KANEMASU AND GYOZO MOLNAR

4 **From past to present: is there room for professional rugby in the United States of America?** 37
LINDSEY GASTON AND LARA KILLICK

5 **Struggling for recognition: developing rugby union in Lebanon** 50
DANYEL REICHE AND AXEL MAUGENDRE

6 **'Moufflons' living precariously: the brief history of rugby union in Cyprus** 64
MIKE RAYNER

7	**Rugby and sport development in Brazil: from peripheral to centre stage**	77
	GARETH HALL AND ARIANNE REIS	
8	**Rugby beyond the core in Africa**	90
	NICHOLAS WISE	
9	**Rugby towards 2030**	104
	JOHN HARRIS	
	Index	115

Figures

8.1　Africa's member unions　　　　　　　　　　　　　95

Tables

2.1	Top four finishers in each Rugby World Cup (1987–2015)	13
4.1	USA Rugby membership in 2018	40
5.1	State of the art of rugby union in Lebanon (February 2019)	54
5.2	Lebanon's squad at the 2018 men's West Asian Division 3 championship	61
7.1	Total number of Rugby players in Brazil, Argentina and Sudámerica Rugby	80
8.1	Africa Cup result fixtures in 2015 and 2016; Gold Cup, Silver Cup and Bronze Cup result fixtures in 2017 and 2018	97
8.2	African nations finishing place in the Women's and Men's Rugby World Cup Sevens competition	99
8.3	Africa Women's and Men's Sevens results since becoming an annual competition	100

Contributors

Lindsey Gaston is a Senior Lecturer in Events Management at Liverpool John Moores University, UK. He holds a PhD in Social Science and Health from Durham University focusing on sports sociology and has conducted research on the social history of rugby.

Gareth Hall is a Senior Lecturer in Psychology at Aberystwyth University, UK. He is a social psychologist with a background in social identity theory and mixed methodologies in applied contexts, focusing on Sport for Development.

John Harris is Associate Dean Research in the Glasgow School for Business and Society at Glasgow Caledonian University. Born in Tredegar (Wales), he is the author of *Rugby Union and Globalization* and was head coach of Kent State University RFC.

Yoko Kanemasu is a Senior Lecturer in Sociology in the School of Social Sciences at the University of the South Pacific, Fiji. She is the author of a series of publications on rugby in Fiji and convenor of 2013 Fiji Rugby Centenary Conference.

Lara Killick is an Assistant Professor in the Department of Kinesiology and Health Promotion at California State Polytechnic University, Pomona, USA. Her research interests include the efficacy of youth participation methodologies and social injustices in sport.

Axel Maugendre is a PhD student at the University of Strasbourg, France working in the field of the sociology of sports. He is also a rugby union player for a Lebanese club and has coached the national Under 18 team.

Gyozo Molnar is a Principal Lecturer in Sport Studies in the School of Sport and Exercise Science at the University of Worcester, UK.

His current publications and research revolve around migration, globalisation, identity and empowering marginalised populations.

Mike Rayner is a Senior Lecturer in Sports Management in the Department of Sport and Exercise Science at the University of Portsmouth, UK. He is the author of *Rugby Union and Professionalisation: Elite Player Perspectives*.

Danyel Reiche is an Associate Professor of Comparative Politics at the American University Beirut, Lebanon, working on sport policy and politics. He is the author of *Success and Failure of Countries at the Olympic Games*.

Arianne Reis is a Senior Lecturer in Leisure and Recreation Studies at Western Sydney University, Australia. Her research focuses on how sport can foster healthy living, environmental awareness and social justice.

Nicholas Wise is a Senior Lecturer in Tourism and Event Management at Liverpool John Moores University. He is the co-editor of seven books and has published widely on sport, tourism and events. Born in Lancaster County (Pennsylvania, USA), he played rugby for Lock Haven University.

Acknowledgements

We would like to thank Simon Whitmore and Rebecca Connor at Routledge for supporting this project. Thanks also to the reviewers who offered constructive comments on the original proposal. All contributors to this collection were a delight to work with. They delivered chapters on time to a tight schedule and provided some fascinating insights into rugby in a variety of different locations. Danielle and Farnaz continued to take care of all the important things while we pushed ahead with our third co-edited collection. Away from the computer screen, Thomas, Iestyn and Noyan keep us busy and have a number of options open to them in the core and on the periphery of international rugby. Allez Allez Allez.

1 Japan 2019 and the internationalisation of rugby union

John Harris and Nicholas Wise

Introduction

The decision to stage the 2019 Rugby World Cup (RWC) in Japan represents a significant moment for the sport as the event takes place outside of the eight foundation nations (Wales, Scotland, South Africa, New Zealand, Ireland, France, England and Australia) for the first time. This collection uses the event as a departure point for looking at rugby union beyond the core of the eight nations listed above to consider the place of the sport in various parts of the periphery. It is important to note from the outset that we do not try to cover every single nation on the periphery within this book as this would require a significantly larger collection than what is provided here. This would also necessarily include a number of nations where to the best of our knowledge there is very little academic research on rugby taking place. In some ways, this book is also a starting point to encourage future research on rugby union in other parts of the world. Drawing upon the work of scholars from a number of disciplinary backgrounds, we aim to discuss and critically assess the positioning of rugby in a variety of different locations. The sub-title of this collection highlights that we are looking specifically at places on the periphery of the rugby world. It is important to state that we do not mean to over-simplify the distinction between core and periphery here, and the next section briefly outlines some of the key factors underpinning our understanding of core and periphery by focusing on the importance of place.

Geographers have directed much attention towards understanding place (see Agnew, 1987; Cresswell, 2015). Academics have also debated conceptual notions of space and place, suggesting that space becomes place not only through experience (e.g. Tuan, 1974) but also through semblances of power, designation and control (e.g. Harvey, 1973). From the scope of the latter understanding, many geographers have reassessed approaches of place to locate countries in relation to other countries based on power structures or governance within rugby union (e.g. Harris and Wise, 2011; Overton, Murray and Heitger, 2013). More recent work has also highlighted the important role that a geographical analysis of sport can provide in contributing to our understanding of broader social issues (see Koch, 2017; Wise, 2015; Wise and Kohe, 2018). Ideas of place change through globalisation, emphasising increased international agendas and fluid movements of people. Agnew and Duncan (1989, p. 1) have also acknowledged the difficulty of defining the term, suggesting place 'can also mean "rank" in a list'. Therefore, this work positions a place as being an abstract location or place(ment) among an already established hierarchal relationship structured by who defines the core and who is regarded as peripheral.

In an earlier text, one of us suggested that given the hegemonic power of a core group of eight nations in the sport, then rugby union consisted largely of a core and a periphery (see Harris, 2010). This acknowledged the notion of a semi-periphery to describe the emerging place of nations such as Italy and Argentina in international rugby and pointed out that some nations were much closer to the core than others (see also Wise, 2017). The wider reference to core and periphery in the text was also based on the dominance of the eight core nations in governance terms (Harris, 2010). In the second decade of the twenty-first century, there has been progress made on extending the involvement of peripheral nations in rugby governance. In 2015 after the RWC in England (and Cardiff), World Rugby reformed its governance structure as outlined in their press release as 'creating a dynamic environment for wider union and regional representation' (World Rugby, 2015). This change afforded wider representation to nations from outside of the core and also recognised the importance of women's rugby as a key part of the future of the sport. Harris (2010, p. 22) commented on the emerging influence of a small group of nations beyond the core and suggested that:

> If rugby is to develop and become more international then it is hoped that future works will be able to document these advances and that accounts will be published concerning those nations who are furthest out on the periphery of the game.

The collection we present here has deliberately brought together a variety of cases of rugby in nations of different sizes and where the sport is at varying stages of development. It is also an attempt to engage with gender issues, the continued growth of rugby sevens and some of the work around sport for development in critically reflecting upon the role that rugby can play as a force for good. As is the case with many academic studies of sport, much of the published work is undertaken by sports fans, and we bring to this collection our own different experiences of rugby as players, coaches, spectators and in a range of other roles. Collectively, we are a group comprising of a variety of different nationalities from both within and outside of the hegemonic core of rugby union. Yet despite many of us being rugby fans and champions of the sport, there must also be space to critically assess the contemporary rugby landscape and to challenge dominant ideologies. Drawing upon literature on the globalisation of sport, and associated scholarship on mega-events, we will first consider just how and why Japan 2019 is such an important moment in the development of rugby as an international sport.

Big in Japan

While Japan 2019 has been widely celebrated as a momentous occasion for international rugby and a very important development for the sport, many felt that this should have taken place eight years earlier. Japan were the favourites to host the 2011 RWC and staging the tournament there would have provided a springboard to the fast-growing Asian economies (Spectrum Value Partners and Addleshaw Goddard, 2008). Awarding the 2011 event to New Zealand, despite the smaller financial return that this would bring, led to Yoshiro Mori of the Japanese Rugby Football Union of accusing those in power of 'passing the ball around their friends'. This seemed like a missed opportunity and that despite the governance rhetoric of growing the game and expanding the international profile of the sport, there was still a tight control exerted over the ball. If the hegemonic core of eight nations were the forward pack, then there seemed to be a reluctance to get the ball out to the backs and move towards a more expansive game (Harris, 2010, 2013). Whatever the pressures and motivations in taking the World Cup to different places, doing so offers a range of opportunities and could introduce the sport to new audiences and develop its international reach. Japan will be the first of the Tier 2 rugby nations to host the RWC, and so this potentially represents a significant moment for the sport if other Tier 2 nations are able to follow this with successful bids to host future tournaments.

Rugby union has a long history in Japan. Richards (2007) noted how the British had played the game in treaty ports for years with a famous picture showing a match from 1874. He highlights how this did not involve locals, but the game was introduced to students at Keio University in 1899 (Richards, 2007). Light (2000) looked at various aspects of the game in Japan and offers an insightful historical account of the ways in which the sport has developed in the country. One of the key features of the sport in the country was the involvement of major corporations who were able to offer a level of financial support that was the envy of rugby clubs in many other nations. In the amateur era then, this provided opportunities for players that were not available in many other nations. In recent years, some of the biggest names in international rugby such as Shane Williams (Wales) and Dan Carter (New Zealand) have taken up lucrative contracts in Japan towards the end of their playing careers. Light, Hirai and Ebishima (2008) highlighted how the changes brought about by globalisation and the professionalisation of rugby led to a decline in the game's popularity as many of the traditions of the sport were eroded. The most recent figures available from World Rugby (2017) suggest that there are over 100,000 registered players in Japan.

The wider terrain of mega-events has long since included Japan as Tokyo was successful in its bid to host the 1964 Olympic Games. The increased commercialisation of the Olympic Games since 1984 (Los Angeles) means that this event is now by far one of the two biggest mega-events. Tokyo is firmly positioned as a world city due to its technological and financial infrastructure that places it at the centre of the world order. The city will host the Olympic Games again in 2020. Coming one year after the RWC, this places Tokyo and Japan at the centre of the mega-events world and points the way for a similar sequence to follow when France hosts the RWC in 2023 and Paris stages the Olympic Games one year after that. Japan was previously chosen as co-host (with South Korea) of the other of the world's two biggest mega-events when it staged the FIFA Football World Cup in 2002. While the 2015 RWC in England was described as being straightforward to stage (Owen, 2015), Japan 2019 has been described by World Rugby as being the most challenging RWC yet due to the inexperience of the organising committee and concerns about stadiums being ready on schedule (Sky Sports, 2018).

Research on the globalisation of sport has often included discussions of Japan given its powerful economic positioning within the global world order. The financial power of leading Japanese businesses such as Sony and Toyota has seen these companies invest significant sums of money in sport. Richards (2007, p. 18) has noted how 'the game's inversion of conventional geopolitics, with Germany, Japan and the

United States as likeable underdogs and New Zealand as a ruthless imperial superpower' highlights the unique shape of rugby.

Japan has appeared in every RWC tournament to date. They suffered heavy defeats to two of the core nations in their group (Australia and England) in the first event but narrowly missed out on a victory against the USA in their other group match. In 1995, the last RWC before rugby went openly professional, Japan set an unwanted record for the most points conceded in a test-match between two nations when they were beaten 145-17 by New Zealand. This match highlighted the huge differences between some of the Tier 1 nations and those in Tier 2. One of the challenges in developing rugby as a more global sport has been the massive gap between the playing power of the highest ranked teams and everyone else. This has meant that it has usually been quite easy to predict, with a certain degree of confidence, which nations would make up the quarter-finalists of each RWC to date.

It should be noted here that only four different nations have ever won a RWC. This is not really that surprising because the development of the game has been rather limited and a tight control has been exerted over the sport by a small group of eight nations (Harris, 2010, 2013; Richards, 2007). Therefore, given these nations have formed the core of the sport, and many of these have been the focus of the work of sport scholars, this timely collection looks at rugby from a global perspective and places the emphasis on those from the semi-periphery and the periphery to assess and critique meanings and development surrounding the sport.

Despite there only being four nations that have won the RWC to date, and qualification into the event is fairly predictable, Japan played (and won) one of the most defining matches in the RWC. In the 2015 RWC, Japan caused one of the biggest upsets in the history of the game when they defeated two-time World Cup winners South Africa in the group stages of the competition. This result attracted widespread media attention across the leading rugby-playing nations and beyond (see Scott, Billings, Harris and Vincent, 2018). It also garnered significant interest for rugby in Japan with the suggestion that this win saw a marked increase in the number of people watching RWC matches on television in the country (see McCurry, 2015). This was particularly important given that any additional exposure for the sport ahead of the 2019 event would be crucial to generating interest in Japan. It is a somewhat recent phenomenon, but there is now a focus on televised sporting events being played in front of capacity crowds with no empty seats in the stadium. Bruce (2013) noted that although central to New Zealand's national sporting identity, filling stadiums at the 2011 RWC was a challenge given a lack of local interest in the event and the high costs and distance of travelling to New Zealand for the event for fans from many of the nations taking part. There is always an extra pressure on the host nation to perform well in a major sporting event on home soil. Up until 2015, no host nation had failed to progress to the knockout stages of the competition although England were defeated by both Wales and Australia to set an unwanted record here in the 2015 RWC. Japan faces a tough task to move beyond the group stages of the 2019 event as they have been drawn in the same pool as Ireland and Scotland. This group also features Samoa who have themselves been involved in RWC upsets before with victories against Wales in 1991 (as Western Samoa) and 1999, and a Russian team also ranked within the top 20 nations in the world (World Rugby, 2019).

On the periphery

Making the international game more competitive and developing the overall reach of the sport is key to the continued international growth of rugby union. World Rugby seem to have made significant strides forward in the last decade and the inclusion of rugby sevens as an Olympic sport is particularly important here. To go beyond the dominant focus on men's rugby and the 15-a-side version of the game, chapters in this collection also include a focus on sevens, women's rugby and rugby as a domain of sport for good.

Stewart and Keech (2017) note how the story of rugby sevens is under-researched and provide a useful account of how this form of the sport has developed and evolved. Of particular note is their discussion of the Hong Kong Sevens and suggest that the international character of the event differentiated it from any other rugby competition 'presenting Asian rugby with a foothold in the international game' (Stewart and Keech, 2017, p. 100). This is an important point and shows how rugby sevens offers a number of potential routes for development that the 15-a-side version of the game cannot. As will be discussed at various points within this collection, the national and regional variations impacting upon the development of rugby in different parts of the world is very important to note when looking at the current positioning and future possibilities for growth and development. Women's rugby has also developed markedly in the last decade. Women competed in the Hong Kong Sevens for the first time in 1997. Both Canada and the USA have been competitive at the elite level and rank above many of the core rugby nations in the rankings for rugby sevens teams.

The chapters in this collection all highlight aspects of the various challenges facing those playing rugby on the periphery. They point to the issues impacting upon development but also evidence the ways in which rugby can be a force for good and bring about change. There are all sorts of programmes across the world using rugby as a means of addressing key social issues. The positive aspects of rugby and the important changes over recent years will be featured at various points in the collection. The national celebration brought about by Fiji's success in the 2016 Olympic Games is a good example of this. This was the first Olympic medal of any kind to be won by Fiji.

We did not wish to impose a particular theoretical framework or specific approach to the discussion of the different cases and wanted to allow contributors to identify the issues that they believed were most important within the particular context they were looking at. This approach allows for a more emergent and inductive analysis of key themes. It also allows for some reflective insights from our contributors drawing (at times) upon their own experiences of the sport within the particular local context that they are writing about.

Outline of this book

Taking the theme of challenging the core as our starting point we begin in Chapter 2 by (re)considering the place of Argentina in international rugby. As we have highlighted elsewhere, this country has – in performance terms – offered the strongest challenge to the status quo on the world stage (Harris and Wise, 2011). Our chapter here develops this earlier work and considers what entering the Rugby Championship in 2012 and having a team compete in the Super Rugby competition since 2016 means for the game in Argentina. It examines the changing landscape of the sport in the country and the wider region and also considers issues such as the movement of players between nations and the politics of international rugby governance. The increasingly influential role of the former Argentina scrum-half Augustin Pichot in his position as Vice Chairman of World Rugby is particularly important to note.

In Chapter 3, Yoko Kanemasu and Gyozo Molnar show how for elite female rugby players in Fiji there are a number of barriers to overcome. These authors have written widely about the broader landscape of the game in earlier work on rugby in Fiji (see Kanemasu and Molnar, 2013). Their contribution here, drawing upon Kanemasu's extensive fieldwork in the country, provides a very important insight into the women's game and reflects upon the challenges faced by the Fiji team as they attempted to qualify for the Women's RWC.

Lindsey Gaston and Lara Killick consider the place of rugby in the USA in Chapter 4 and focus on the specific challenge of creating a professional league for rugby union. The USA is a core nation in most (broader) discussions of globalisation when addressing economic impacts and political influence, but where we consider rugby and the USA, the country remains somewhat peripheral in some aspects of sport in global perspective. This chapter analyses some of the recent work in developing a professional league within a crowded marketplace where established leagues in other sports assume a hegemonic positioning.

We then turn our attention to two small nations rarely featured in considerations of sport in a global perspective. In Chapter 5, Danyel Reiche and Axel Maugendre examine the place of rugby union in Lebanon. This country has only very recently seen some development in rugby union with a greater focus there on the sport of rugby league. Their contribution here, based on interviews with a number of those involved in the sport within this small country, considers the ways in which the two rugby codes should work closer together. Mike Rayner then looks at the game in Cyprus in Chapter 6, where he documents the important role of the British military in developing the game on the island. This case offers some analysis of the ways in which key stakeholders need to find ways to ensure that the sport has a sustainable future in Cyprus. Both of these chapters offer fascinating insights into places far out on the periphery in the international rugby world and draw our attention to the challenges involved for small nations with a limited number of registered players in securing status as full member nations of World Rugby.

The important role that rugby can play in the domain of sport for good is then discussed by Gareth Hall and Arianne Reis in Chapter 7. Drawing upon fieldwork undertaken in Brazil, they show us how rugby can be a force for good and a means of reaching disadvantaged communities. Hall and Reis also remind us of the particular challenges in developing rugby in a country where football is so popular and examine some of the ways in which sport can be used to engage with different groups. Chapter 8 expands our thinking around core and periphery in a broader discussion of rugby in Africa. Here Nicholas Wise employs aspects of the geographical imagination to examine some of the key places where the sport has developed beyond the core nation of South Africa. This chapter looks at the African Cup series, the underdevelopment of women's rugby and the potential of sevens to shape the future direction of the sport in Africa. In the final chapter, John Harris brings together some of the key themes explored in this book and looks ahead to how rugby may have changed by 2030. This chapter also offers a brief discussion of some places not included as case studies in this collection but locations that are important to the continued development of rugby in a global perspective. Here the case of Italy and the emerging significance of Georgia are looked at as challengers to the established core in Europe. Drawing upon the work of Raymond Williams, Harris also looks to the future as part of a 'journey of hope' for rugby union to develop further on the periphery over the next decade.

Moving forward

Richards (2007, p. 288) suggested that rugby union's 'sheer complexity and range of specialist skills, both individual and collective, always were a barrier to its adoption and growth'. It is a sport that 'only the "committed" could appreciate' (Horton, 2009, p. 969) given some of the complex laws and violent nature. Yet the game is changing. One of the reviewers of our proposal observed that this text seemed to be a contribution offering new perspectives rather than a comprehensive overview of rugby on the periphery. This was always our intention and we hope that the various cases discussed in the pages that follow offer some useful insights into the sport at different levels and stages of development.

The cultural theorist Raymond Williams, who played rugby as a schoolboy in Abergavenny, once suggested that sport was one of the very best things on television and that he would keep his television set for sport alone (Williams, 1968). Williams was only alive for the first RWC and would have had to get up early to view any of the action. One of us (John Harris) set an alarm clock to watch some of these matches before heading to school in Wales. The other (Nicholas Wise), who was only four years old at the time of the first RWC, would not have been able to watch any of the inaugural event as it was not screened in the USA. Nicholas's initial awareness of the event came in 2002 as an exchange student in Springwood, Australia, where he was first introduced to the sport. Since then, he has followed coverage of rugby around the world and watched the 2015 RWC while living in Taiwan.

Japan 2019 is expected to play a key role going forward in terms of commercialising rugby in Asia and beyond. The tournament will be screened in a number of nations across the globe and moves the sport into new territory. With strategic investment in the sport in Asia, Africa and the Americas, we will expect to see more focus on the periphery as the sport expands its boundaries beyond the tight grip and control of the eight core unions. Taking the game forward, those involved in its governance will focus on specific emerging and peripheral nations, the women's game and the development of sevens as an Olympic sport. Rugby has historically been a game for players of all shapes and sizes. While the top level of the international game may be moving away from that, the contributors to this collection show that rugby continues to be important in nations of all shapes and sizes.

References

Agnew, J. (1987). *Place and politics*. Boston, MA: Allen & Unwin.
Agnew, J., and Duncan, J. (1989). *The power of the place: Bringing together geographical and sociological imaginations*. London: Routledge.
Bruce, T. (2013). (Not) a stadium of four million: Speaking back to dominant discourses of the Rugby World Cup in New Zealand. *Sport in Society*, 16(7), 899–911.
Cresswell, T. (2015). *Place: A short introduction* (2nd ed.). Oxford: Blackwell.
Harris, J. (2010). *Rugby union and globalization: An odd-shaped world*. Basingstoke: Palgrave Macmillan.
Harris, J. (2013). Definitely maybe: Continuity and change in the Rugby World Cup. *Sport in Society*, 16(7), 853–862.
Harris, J., and Wise, N. (2011). Geographies of scale in international rugby union. *Geographical Research*, 49(4), 475–483.
Harvey, D. (1973). *Social justice and the city*. Baltimore, MD: Johns Hopkins University Press.
Horton, P. (2009). Rugby union football in Australian society: An unintended consequence of intended action. *Sport in Society*, 12(7), 967–985.
Kanemasu, Y., and Molnar, G. (2013). Pride of the people: Fijian rugby labour migration and collective identity. *International Review for the Sociology of Sport*, 48(6), 720–735.
Koch, N. (2017) (Ed.) *Critical geographies of sport: Space, power, and sport in global perspective*. London: Routledge.
Light, R. (2000). A centenary of rugby and masculinity in Japanese schools and universities: Continuity and change. *Sporting Traditions*, 16, 87–104.
Light, R., Hirai, H., and Ebishima, H. (2008). Tradition, identity, professionalism and tensions in Japanese rugby. In G. Ryan (Ed.) *The changing face of rugby: The union game and professionalism since 1995*. Newcastle: Cambridge Scholars Publishing (pp. 147–164).
McCurry, J. (2015). Japan's Rugby World Cup success breaks world TV viewing record. Available at www.theguardian.com/sport/2015/oct/06/japans-rugby-world-cup-success-breaks-world-tv-viewing-record
Overton, J., Murray, W., and Heitger, J. (2013). Pass the passport! Geographies of the Rugby World Cup 2011. *New Zealand Geographer*, 69(2), 94–107.
Owen, D. (2015). Global goals get a commercial kicker. *FT Rugby*, September 10.

Richards, H. (2007). *A game for hooligans: The history of rugby union.* Edinburgh: Mainstream.

Scott, O., Billings, A., Harris, J., and Vincent, J. (2018). Using self-categorization theory to uncover the framing of the 2015 Rugby World Cup: A cross-cultural comparison of three nations' newspapers. *International Review for the Sociology of Sport*, 53(8), 997–1015.

Sky Sports (2018). 2019 Rugby World Cup in Japan the most difficult to organise, says World Rugby. Available at www.skysports.com/rugby-union/news/12337/11502325/2019-rugby-world-cup-in-japan-the-most-difficult-to-organise-says-world-rugby

Spectrum Value Partners and Addleshaw Goddard (2008). *Putting rugby first: An independent report into rugby's global future.* London: Spectrum Value Partners and Addleshaw Goddard.

Stewart, J., and Keech, M. (2017). The globalization of rugby sevens: From novelty to the Olympic Games. In J. Nauright and T. Collins (Eds.) *The rugby world in the professional era.* London: Routledge (pp. 93–107).

Tuan, Y.-F. (1974). *Topophilia.* Englewood Cliffs, NJ: Prentice-Hall.

Williams, R. (1968). As we see others. *The Listener*, August 1.

Wise, N. (2015). Geographical approaches and the sociology of sport. In R. Giulianotti (Ed.) *Routledge handbook of the sociology of sport.* London: Routledge (pp. 142–152).

Wise, N. (2017). Rugby World Cup: New directions or more of the same? *Sport in Society*, 20(3), 341–354.

Wise, N., and Kohe, G. (2018). Sports geography: New approaches, perspectives and directions. *Sport in Society* (Online first). Doi: 10.1080/17430437.2018.1555209

World Rugby (2015). Expanded game representation and independence at the heart of World Rugby governance reform. Available at www.world.rugby/news/122987

World Rugby (2017). Player numbers. Available at www.world.rugby/development/player-numbers?lang=en

World Rugby (2019). Men's rankings. Available at www.world.rugby/rankings/mru?lang=en

2 Challenging the core
The rise of Argentina in international rugby

Nicholas Wise and John Harris

Introduction

This chapter looks at the place of Argentina in the international rugby landscape and considers the role they have to play in developing the game in the Southern Hemisphere more generally. Geographical notions of scale and core/periphery are applied to this case as a means of further understanding where the nation 'fits' in the international rugby world. Argentina's third-place finish at the 2007 Rugby World Cup (RWC), where they became the only team from outside the founding eight nations to place in the top four of the competition, was a key moment for the international game. After their success in 2007, Argentina was able to push for more regular international test matches against the core nations in the Southern Hemisphere and now compete in The Rugby Championship. Argentina have struggled to match their opponents on the field and have finished bottom of the table almost every year between 2012 and 2018 (the exception being in 2015 when they edged out South Africa on points difference). Yet it should be noted here that at the 2015 RWC in England, Argentina finished fourth in a tournament where all of the semi-finalists came from the Southern Hemisphere. The dominance of New Zealand, South Africa and Australia within the RWC, together with the emerging power of Argentina, can be seen in Table 2.1 (note also that South Africa did not compete in the first two RWC competitions).

Argentina has played in every one of the eight RWC competitions to date and will be looking for another strong performance in 2019. Argentina had to wait some time for the opportunity to be a part of an international competition like The Rugby Championship and to be supported to have a professional team located in the country to compete in Super Rugby. Given the focus of this book on rugby outside of the hegemonic core, this chapter offers insight into Argentina's rise

Table 2.1 Top four finishers in each Rugby World Cup (1987–2015)

World Cup	Winner	Runner-up	3rd Place	4th Place
1987	New Zealand	France	Wales	Australia
1991	Australia	England	New Zealand	Scotland
1995	South Africa	New Zealand	France	England
1999	Australia	France	South Africa	New Zealand
2003	England	Australia	New Zealand	France
2007	South Africa	England	**Argentina**	France
2011	New Zealand	France	Australia	Wales
2015	New Zealand	Australia	South Africa	**Argentina**

and how they have challenged the established nations of the rugby world more than any other country.

Similar to other nations, rugby in Argentina sits in the shadow of the more dominant sport of football. Argentina won the FIFA Football World Cup in 1978 and 1986, and the sport is an important signifier of Argentinean identity where its leading male players can become national heroes (see Archetti, 2001). Research on rugby and Argentina has received far less attention in the academic literature. They were the only nation from the top ten teams in the world who were not the focus of a chapter in Ryan's (2008) edited collection detailing the changes in rugby since open professionalisation in 1995. Argentina does not feature in the more recent collection of work by rugby scholars looking at a longer period of professional rugby union (Nauright and Collins, 2017).

We have attempted to outline the position of Argentina in relation to core/periphery relations within the sport (Harris and Wise, 2011, 2012). While this offered an initial geographical analysis of international rugby, it is important to look at what has happened in the last seven years and to allow us to consider what more recent changes have meant for the sport in the country. Before moving on to discuss contemporary issues, the next section briefly outlines the history of rugby in Argentina to provide some context for the discussion that follow.

A brief history of rugby union in Argentina

In the mid-1860s, many Britons moved to Argentina to invest in the economic potential of the Pampas, and British stockholders had a strong involvement in the railroad network being constructed during that time. While Argentina was not part of the British Empire, the country had strong commercial links with Britain, and English cricket clubs were noted to have moved rugby's development forward in many countries around the world (Richards, 2007). This is still evident today, as rugby is commonly played in railroad towns beyond Buenos Aires such as Mendoza and Rosario as a result of the British legacy (Unión Argentina de Rugby, 2008). The first rugby match in Argentina took place in 1873, with participation encouraged by British immigrants.

Argentina's rugby governing body was formed in 1899. The formation was a result of mergers between four clubs: Belgrano Athletic, Buenos Aires Rugby Football Club, Lomas Athletic and Rosario Athletic. This group is formerly known as the Unión de Rio de la Plata (Unión Argentina de Rugby, 2008), representing a formation of clubs from the Rio de la Plata and Buenos Aires region. In 1910, Argentina held their first international match in Buenos Aires, competing against a touring British team, and travelled to neighbouring Chile in 1936 where they played (and won) their first match on foreign soil (Unión Argentina de Rugby, 2008). The original club name, Unión de Rio de la Plata, was changed to the Unión Argentina de Rugby in 1951 to put emphasis on the nation. This was also the same year Argentina hosted the South American Rugby Tournament against Brazil, Chile and Uruguay (Unión Argentina de Rugby, 2008). Argentina continued to host teams from Europe through the 1950s/1960s, and in 1965 made their first transatlantic tour to South Africa. World Rugby (2016) figures suggest that there are over 100,000 registered players in Argentina.

International rugby governance and strategy: positioning Argentina

Academics from across the world have looked at various aspects of international sport governance, and the research in this area has developed markedly in the period since rugby went openly professional (e.g. Hums and MacLean, 2018). Yet despite these advances, little work has considered sport governance in relation to rugby or particularly around key geographical issues shaping the sport in a global perspective. Rugby is also notably absent from many discussions about the wider policy issues within global sport, and the game will often not even warrant an entry into the index of sport management texts on the subject. The hegemonic positioning of the two most 'mega' of the mega-events (the summer Olympic Games and men's Football World Cup) has attracted the attention of scholars across the world for many years (e.g. Roche, 2000; Tomlinson and Whannel, 1984). When we consider the RWC, there have been some claims that this is the third biggest global sporting event (see Harris, 2010, 2013; Hutchins and Phillips, 1999; Wise, 2017), but this remains a contested space and other events also stake a claim to that position (see Harris, Skillen and McDowell, 2017).

As noted in the introduction to this collection, the governance of rugby union has been dominated by the eight foundation member nations. The governance of international rugby, as with many other sports, has in recent years focused in large part on developing the game as the increased commercialisation and commodification of the sports business has assumed an increasingly important role. More opportunities to develop the game in countries such as Argentina are based on the International Rugby Board's (now known as World Rugby) 2010–2020 strategy to develop and invest in specific places outside of the eight core nations (International Rugby Board, 2010).

In their strategic plan, the governing body noted that 'ensuring Argentina's participation in an expanded Tri-Nations tournament is successful' was integral to ongoing expansion developments of the game – to make rugby a truly international sport (International Rugby Board, 2010). This first step has been accomplished with Argentina participating in The Rugby Championship since 2012. Argentina is still dependent upon World Rugby decisions when it comes to dedicating efforts and finances to support future expansion of Argentinean rugby. The next wave of expansion came in 2016 with a professional Super Rugby team (Buenos Aires Los Jaguares). Argentina has just completed their seventh year of competition in The Rugby Championship and are in a very different position to when we first looked at the positioning of the nation within the global rugby landscape (see Harris and Wise, 2011). Argentina have new influence based on solid international performances on the field of play, inclusion in elite competition and the increasingly prominent role of former national team captain Augustín Pichot as Vice Chairman of World Rugby. Pichot, who represented Argentina 71 times as a player, was in 2016 described by *Rugby World* magazine as the most influential man in the whole of world rugby.

Assessing Argentina's rise

This chapter contributes to the sports geography literature by bringing together notions of place framed alongside a focus on the governance of international rugby to better identify how Argentina is now positioned. The geographical notion of 'place' is used to designate and conceptualise Argentina's position in relation to the global core of the rugby world. Referring to place as a rank, or hierarchy, helps explain how rugby governance influences (and has limited)

Argentina's emergent position or interconnected place in a global system. This consideration thus expands on understandings of 'place' as a conceptual point within hierarchal relationships. As noted in the previous chapter, there is an already developed place(ment) of rugby nations that has long exerted a tight control over the sport.

Argentina are ranked tenth in the world rankings (April 2019), but have been ranked as high as three following the 2007 RWC. It must be noted that the rankings are always changing but Argentina has been consistently ranked among the top ten teams in the world over the past decade. Japan 2019 represents the first time that a nation from outside of the core group will host the RWC competition. In 2016, the President of Argentina announced that Argentina would put forward a bid to host the 2027 RWC.

To critically frame the directions that will be discussed in subsequent sections of this chapter, common geographic terminology identifying scale, core and periphery further positions the conceptual 'place' of Argentina among the rugby playing nations in a global perspective before focusing on the more recent developments since 2012. Notions of scale in relation to core and periphery offer insight into how places are conceptually positioned in relation to others (Herod, 2011; Smith, 1993; Swyngedouw, 1997). The ideas of core and periphery are important here because they are central to the culture of global rugby, and the concept of scale attempts to clarify core/periphery relationships. Moreover, Smith's (1993) idea of 'jumping scales' critically acknowledges the conceptual complexities regarding the challenges Argentina faces if the country is to ascend and join the existing core member nations. According to Swyngedouw (1997, p. 168), 'transformation is accompanied by transgressions of scale boundaries' and leads to the production and restructuring of others.

To conceptualise the place of Argentina in a global rugby perspective, the country's isolation within the sport must first be acknowledged. Many of the elite Argentina players were committed to professional contracts in Europe during the first two decades of open professionalism, as they had the opportunity to earn higher salaries and gain experience in established leagues. As is also the case for many other national rugby federations, this often meant it was challenging to always get these players released for international competition. Today, with the creation of a Super Rugby team in Buenos Aires, many of those who represent the Argentinean national team play for Los Jaguares. If we consider the regional scale, Argentina could be perceived as a regional core in South/Latin America. Their success positions them geographically to further develop the game in South

America. They also represent the most likely candidate to further diffuse the growth of the sport in neighbouring countries with established national rugby unions including Uruguay, Paraguay, Chile and Brazil. These countries may also benefit from Argentina's success in the global context as more resources are directed towards the region.

In rugby union, the core exerts tight control over the vast majority of wealth and power, leading to an uneven distribution of power (see Harris, 2010; Richards, 2007). Argentina has been described as being part of a very small semi-periphery in rugby, or an emerging country, in a global perspective (e.g. Herod, 2011; Wise, 2017). Harris and Wise (2011) adopted Wallerstein's (1974) world systems theory to highlight the significant differences between 'core' and 'periphery' in the movement of athletes between nations. Wallerstein's (1974) widely used approach, based on a neo-Marxist critique of globalisation, provides valuable insights into the inter-relationships of different nations, but it is important to note here that some nations who are on the periphery in economic terms may occupy the core of a particular sporting world (see Harris, 2010; Wise, 2017).

Harris (2010), in an initial attempt to conceptualise the positioning of rugby in a global perspective, suggested that it was probably more apt to refer solely to a core and a periphery when discussing international rugby given the power of the eight foundation unions. While acknowledging Wallerstein's (1974) use of the semi-periphery, it is suggested that if we were to employ this term in rugby, then in some ways, only two nations (Argentina and Italy) would form this group (Harris, 2010). In relation to the governance of the game, the fact that these nations did not receive the voting privileges of the eight foundation unions meant that they were still peripheral in many respects. The changes to the voting rights on the World Rugby Council, agreed after the 2015 RWC, was an important step to involve more nations in the growth of the game.

The Rugby Championship

When Argentina joined the expanded Southern Hemisphere Tri-Nations competition, The Rugby Championship, there was much talk around the importance of the inclusion of a fourth team. Greg Peters, CEO of SANZAR noted that 'the invitation to Argentina to join the Championship is a defining moment for Southern Hemisphere rugby and significant for world rugby' (*The Irish Times*, 2011). Peters added that Argentina's inclusion was long overdue, and they had proven themselves in international competition and they added something new to the existing competition between Australia, New Zealand and South Africa. Argentina's success at the 2007 RWC showed that they had potential to compete with the best teams in the world. But as power relations would dictate, it is not simply about performances on the field of play, but the ability to generate revenue and new commercial gains. While there were clearly some stakeholders pushing the incorporation of Argentina to further develop the sport in that country, there was also emphasis on the need to expand the pre-existing Tri-Nations competition to benefit Australia, New Zealand and South Africa. The focus on a more international approach to rugby governance and the development of the sport is not based solely on growing the game in the periphery but is also shaped by allowing the core nations to expand coverage and generate further commercial revenue. Moving into the South American market and trying to capitalise on the sports growing popularity, there was a strategic move as those involved in the governance of the tournament recognised the need to grow the competition.

Pichot, the former Argentina scrum-half and then UAR's SANZAR Representative, played an important role supporting Argentina's inclusion in The Rugby Championship and noted that 'after many years of history and the hard work of many generations of players on and off the pitch, Argentinean rugby will be part of the toughest and most prestigious tournament in the Southern Hemisphere' (in Rugby Football History, 2011). Building on Pichot's comment, the President of the UAR, Luis Castillo, described much pride in his country's inclusion and stated that they 'will work to maintain high standards in our rugby, with our ultimate goal being to keep generating resources for the development of rugby at the clubs' (Rugby Football History, 2011). Furthermore, Manuel Galindo (UAR High Performance Chairman) stressed this as a significant point in history because Argentina had 'been seeking to participate regularly in a tournament like this' for years (Rugby Football History, 2011). Pichot, Castillo and Galindo each saw The Rugby Championship as Argentina finding their place in the global rugby landscape. For Argentina, inclusion was about opportunity, while for SANZAR, it was about delivering an improved product. This is where geographical interpretations are necessary because the 'placing' of a country strategically aligns with product and power.

Argentina is in a position to develop the game and capture interest in the wider context of South America (especially in places such as Chile, Uruguay and Brazil where the game has seen growth in recent years). Moreover, as noted previously, Argentina are not competing with Australia, New Zealand and South Africa for players so represent less of a threat to the existing hegemonies in place.

SANZAAR and Super Rugby

From 2016, two major developments would bring Argentina in line with those at the core of rugby governance in the Southern Hemisphere. First, SANZAR would become South Africa, New Zealand, Australia and Argentina Rugby (SANZAAR). Second, as noted earlier in this chapter, Argentina was awarded a Super Rugby franchise. Despite their newly established presence, the Jaguares compete in the South Africa conference. This highlights some of the challenges in developing the game in the Southern Hemisphere and the logistical challenges involved in playing matches over such a large geographical area. Pichot's increasingly influential position in World Rugby gave the country a stronger voice and international presence in global rugby governance. Pichot continues to play a pivotal role in ensuring Argentina and other nations from outside of the core are able to have more of a voice in the direction of future developments.

The formation of SANZAAR helped lay the foundation for Argentina as part of the core of professional rugby in the Southern Hemisphere. Initially Argentina was being considered for two professional teams (*The Guardian*, 2013), but to spread the development of the sport, it was decided that one team would be based in Argentina and the other in Japan (Super Rugby, 2014). Having a professional team in the country bringing many of the leading players together would mean that members of the national team would be playing together more often. Agusten Creevy, the Jaguares captain in 2016, noted that:

> It will help us not only to become a more unified team, but also to provide the group with continuity. We will now have the chance to keep on growing as individuals, to get to know each other much better as to the game and to become a better team as a whole.
> (Super XV, 2015)

In 2015, the inclusion of an Argentinean-based team in Super Rugby meant that the Jaguares were able to attract and sign key players who represent the national team. Having a professional team in Argentina is very important to any future growth, but it must also be noted that the economic core remains located in the Northern Hemisphere (see Super Rugby, 2018). Even the three leading Southern Hemisphere nations have had to face up to the fact that some of their top players would move to England or France at an earlier age than had been the case in the past. This has led to some national federations making changes to the criteria used for players to be eligible for national teams and some players have been selected for their country while playing overseas (in the past by moving to play in another country they would not have been considered for selection for the national team). But in terms of developing the game in Argentina, Pichot noted that 'since we started with this project of insertion in the game's elite, at the end of 2007, it was crucial to have regular competition for our players' (in Super Rugby, 2014).

There was a clear need from a geographical standpoint to develop a strictly Southern Hemisphere competition, despite Argentina historically being more successful against the core European nations (when discussions about including Argentina in one of the elite competitions first commenced). What seemed to initially result as an attempt to incorporate Argentina and gain from commercial revenue in a growing rugby region and market has a positive future outlook. Beginning in 2016, an established professional team has potential to develop more talent, allow domestic supporters to view more top-level matches and television rights will bring more money to aid in developing the sport. Argentina's more established presence in 2016 points to an emerging challenge to the core that also includes a first RWC outside of the foundation nations when Japan hosts the 2019 event.

Argentina did not have voting power in SANZAR until 2016 when the organisation became SANZAAR. Before their full inclusion, Argentina was dependent on the policies and regulations of SANZAR. While Argentina are a new member and have one team in the Super Rugby competition, they are in a much more significant and strategic position compared to the start of the decade when we first looked at Argentina's place in international rugby (Harris and Wise, 2011, 2012). Here we discussed Argentina's status geographically as part of the semi-periphery and that has since evolved to the present time where they now have voting rights as a full member of SANZAAR, making the shift from being dependent to having a greater say in shaping the future direction and decisions of international rugby.

The future

As they attempted to find a place among the core rugby nations, given their future was dependent on the voting powers of the founding eight members and the future directions of SANZAR, Argentina faced quite a challenge to move closer to the core. There is a chance that the future expansion of Super Rugby will lead to Argentina having two professional teams in the coming years. This development, and the support of Pichot within World Rugby governance circles, could mean that they are in a strong position to put in a bid to host the 2027 RWC. The changing landscape has also reconfigured where many of the top Argentinean rugby players now play their club rugby and earn their salaries. The movement of elite players back to Argentina with an established Super Rugby club in Buenos Aires may help the sport to grow domestically. If managed correctly, this will allow much better access to players for those running the national team and a coordinated approach to player welfare ensuring that the top players are not asked to play too many matches each season.

Argentina continues to benefit from playing against the most successful teams in the world and are themselves now in a more influential position to contribute to future growth. Many of the squad selected for the Argentina national team in the 2018–2019 season played for the Jaguares. It is also important to note here that an Argentina XV also competes in the Americas Rugby Championship. The team that competes in the Americas Rugby Championship is the second (or development) team below the Pumas and provides an opportunity for players to make the step up to international rugby. In 2019, Argentina were once again the winners of this competition and did not lose a single match. Argentina also hosts the World Under 20 Championship for the second time in June, 2019 with matches taking place in Rosario and Santa Fe. Having staged the event in 2010, the 2019 tournament could provide an important opportunity for the host nation to match (or better) their third-place finish in 2016. Buenos Aires hosted the 2018 (Summer) Youth Olympics and Argentina took the rugby sevens title in the boys competition.

The notion of place in this chapter has been discussed as a position, rank or hierarchy in a global system where the established hierarchy within rugby union controlled the direction and development of the sport. Argentina has marked their presence in the global rugby landscape but has in some ways yet to be given a defined place. Argentina will play in The Rugby Championship for the eighth year running, SANZAR is now SANZAAR, the Buenos Aires Jaguares compete in Super Rugby and Pichot is Vice Chairman of World Rugby. There has clearly been significant development since we first looked at the place of Argentina in the wider international rugby landscape (Harris and Wise, 2011).

As will be discussed at various points in this collection, the inclusion of rugby sevens in the Olympic Games represents an important moment in the increased internationalisation of the sport. The fact that rugby made its debut in 2016, at the Olympiad in Rio de Janeiro, was another boost for rugby in South America. Argentina's men's squad qualified for the Rio Olympics but were eliminated by Great Britain and Northern Ireland in the quarter-finals. Argentina did not have a team compete in the women's event at Rio, as they were knocked out of the Olympics Repechage tournament by Russia, but it is in the sevens version of the sport that the country has made some inroads into developing women's rugby. Argentina's national sevens team is often considered to be the second most successful team from the region in women's rugby after Brazil. The country does not have a 15-a-side team in the World Rankings for women's rugby but has played in a World Sevens Series event. As is the case in many other nations, both in the core and on the periphery, rugby has long been positioned as a masculine game, and women have faced many challenges in getting involved in the sport.

The next few years represent a challenging and interesting time for the sport as those involved in its governance pursue an internationalisation agenda to develop the game beyond the narrow core. Argentina has pointed the way forward for other nations to show that they can challenge the dominant nations. Yet it may be in sevens rugby and/or women's rugby that more sustained challenges will be made. The tight grip of the core will need to loosen some more if the sport is to see other countries rise among the ranks of international rugby in the way that Argentina have done.

References

Archetti, E. (2001). The spectacle of a heroic life: The case of Diego Maradona. In D. Andrews and S. Jackson (Eds.) *Sports stars: The cultural politics of sporting celebrity*. London: Routledge (pp. 151–164).

Harris, J. (2010). *Rugby Union and globalization: An odd-shaped world*. Basingstoke: Palgrave Macmillan.

Harris, J. (2013). Definitely maybe: Continuity and change in the Rugby World Cup. *Sport in Society*, 16(7), 853–862.

Harris, J., Skillen, F., and McDowell, M. (2017). Introduction: The contested terrain of major sporting events. *Sport in Society*, 20(3), 325–327.

Harris, J., and Wise, N. (2011). Geographies of scale in international rugby union—the case of Argentina. *Geographical Research*, 49(4), 375–383.

Harris, J., and Wise, N. (2012). The place of Argentina in international rugby: Between and beyond core and periphery. In A. Rossi and L. Maranda (Eds.) *Argentina: Environmental, geographical and cultural issues*. Hauppague: Nova Science.

Herod, A. (2011). *Scale (key ideas in geography)*. London: Routledge.

Hums, M., and MacLean, J. (2018). *Governance and policy in sport organizations* (4th ed.). London: Routledge.

Hutchins, B., and Phillips, M.G. (1999). The global union: globalization and the Rugby World Cup. In T. Chandler and J. Nauright (Eds.) *Making the rugby world: race, gender, commerce*. London: Cass (pp. 149–164).

International Rugby Board (2010). *Strategic plan 2010–2020*. Dublin: International Rugby Board.

Nauright, J., and Collins, T. (Eds.) (2017). *The rugby world in the professional era*. London: Routledge.

Roche, M. (2000). *Mega-events and modernity: Olympics and expos in the growth of global culture*. London: Routledge.

Richards, H. (2007). *A game for hooligans: The history of rugby union*. Edinburgh: Mainstream.

Ryan, G. (Ed.) (2008). *The changing face of rugby: The union game and professionalism since 1995*. Newcastle: Cambridge Scholars Publishing.

Rugby Football History (2011). Rugby Championship. Available at www.rugbyfootballhistory.com/rugby_championship.html

Smith, N. (1993). Homeless/global: Scaling places. In J. Bird, B. Curtis, T. Putnam, G. Robertson and L. Tickner (Eds.) *Mapping the futures: Local cultures, global change*. London: Routledge.

Super Rugby (2014). Japan and Argentina officially joint Super Rugby. Available at https://super.rugby/superrugby/news/japan-and-argentina-officially-join-super-rugby/

Super Rugby (2018). 'Speedy Gonzalo' returns to Argentina as Jaguares coach. Available at www.rugby.com.au/news/2018/08/09/super-rugby-jaguares-coach-2019

Super XV (2015). Argentina reveal Jaguars Super Rugby team. Available at www.superxv.com/argentina-reveal-jaguars-super-rugby-team/#ixzz5fA7BKUv6

Swyngedouw, E. (1997). Excluding the other: The production of scale and scaled politics. In R. Lee and J. Wills (Eds.) *Geographies of economies*. London: Arnold (pp. 167–177).

The Guardian (2013). Super Rugby may accept Argentinian teams in 2016. Available at www.theguardian.com/sport/2013/aug/08/super-rugby-considers-argentinian-teams

The Irish Times (2011). Pumas debut against Springboks. Available at www.irishtimes.com/sport/rugby/pumas-debut-against-springboks-1.1285661

Tomlinson, A., and Whannel, G. (1984). *Five ring circus: Money, power and politics at the Olympic Games*. London: Pluto Press.

Unión Argentina de Rugby (2008). Hechos salientes de la historica del rugby internacional y nacional. Available at www.uar.com.ar/conte01.asp?tx1=gri18&ti1=momen&ti2=Momentos%20Históricos

Wallerstein, I. (1974). *The modern world system, Volume 1*. New York: Academic Press.

Wise, N. (2017). Rugby World Cup: New directions or more of the same? *Sport in Society*, 20(3), 341–354.

World Rugby (2016). Global rugby participation. Available at www.world.rugby/development/player-numbers?lang=en

3 Against all odds

Fijiana's flight from zero to hero in the Rugby World Cup

Yoko Kanemasu and Gyozo Molnar

Introduction

Rugby union is widely recognised as Fiji's most popular sport, which is 'in every Fijian's blood' (Ramsay, 2018). First introduced to the country in the late nineteenth century under British colonial rule, rugby is played by approximately 80,000 people (out of a population of 885,000), reportedly 'the highest player-population ratio of any rugby playing nation' (Fiji Rugby Union (FRU), 2019). Fijian players' 'natural flair' and physical abilities, as well as rugby's embeddedness in local culture/indigenous tradition, have been frequently commented on.

Rugby's symbolic power in Fiji was most vividly displayed in 2016, when the men's national sevens side won the county's first-ever Olympic Gold Medal. Following the final match, the nation erupted, with a special public holiday declared, a FJ$7 banknote issued and an official ceremony held to honour the team. Roads leading up to the stadium where the ceremony was held were filled with national flags, people wearing blue (colour of the national flag), with joyous singing and shouting – creating an impromptu citizens' parade. The crowd gathered at the stadium to witness the team being congratulated by Fiji's president and other dignitaries.

Given the game's hyper-popularity, rugby has attracted considerable research attention in recent years. Anthropological studies highlight the indigenised nature of the sport, through intricate linkages with indigenous martial tradition and ideals of communality, spirituality and masculinity (e.g. Presterudstuen, 2010). Researchers have also explored rugby's symbolic role as a cultural marker of ethno-national identity as well as its exclusion of non-indigenous Fijians and deployment for political purposes (Cattermole, 2008; Guinness and Besnier, 2016; Kanemasu and Molnar, 2013a). Much of the existing research has shown how 'rugby has come to symbolise the reconstituted Fijian notion of tradition and ethno-national identity in which the pre-modern and the colonial have merged into a Fijianness' (Presterudstuen, 2010, p. 242) in the country's postcolonial context based on dominant cultural discourses and ethno-racial power relations.

In the shadow of this conspicuous rugby discourse are alternative voices that illuminate further power dynamics of rugby (as a social practice) in Fiji. A small community of indigenous Fijian women have actively pursued the game since the late 1980s, with little institutional or community support until recently. Limited research attention has been paid to these athletes, many of whom are gender-non-conforming women, and to what their rugby pursuit means in the context of gender and heteronormativity enforced in and through the game in Fiji (Kanemasu and Johnson, 2019; Kanemasu, Johnson and Molnar, 2018; Kanemasu and Molnar, 2013b, 2015). Studies have examined the consolidation of gendered and heteronormative rugby discourse by its articulation with anti-imperialist nationalism and traditionalism, the struggles and victories of women athletes who challenge this rugby discourse, and grassroots community reactions to their claim to the game. Yet, multiple dimensions and further complexities of their rugby quest remain largely under-investigated.

Throughout the long years of their struggle, qualifying for a Rugby World Cup (RWC) has been a primary goal for the national team – a goal yet to be achieved. In this chapter, we seek to explore women rugby players' engagement with the Women's RWC to contribute to the emerging literature and further illuminate the subjugated (yet resistant) voices of women rugby players in Fiji. This chapter is based on primary data collected in 2016 with six national squad members and the Head Coach. The first author traced the Fijiana's attempt at qualification for the 2017 Women's RWC by assisting with their preparation camp arrangements, regularly visiting/filming the camp, following them to the qualifier matches in Hong Kong and joining their team/prayer meetings before/during the games. This chapter is based on primary data collected in 2016 and 2019 with nine national squad members, two women's rugby officials, and the Head Coach. We present a brief history of the women's pursuit of the game under Fiji's postcolonial conditions and explore what it means to the women to qualify for a RWC in this context. Finally, we examine the local and global relations of power that they are up against in achieving their dream of RWC qualification.

Women's rugby in Fiji

To appreciate the socio-political significance of Fijian women's pursuit of rugby, it is essential to contextualise it in the country's prevailing gender and sexual order. Several indicators point to the profoundly heteropatriarchal nature of Fijian society – such as a low Gender Gap Index (106th of 149 countries), some of the world's highest gender-based violence rates, and prevalent homophobia and transphobia (Fiji Women's Crisis Centre, 2013; World Economic Forum, 2018). Rugby has taken on an intensely gendered and heteronormative nature in this context. This is further consolidated by entrenched traditionalism as well as anti-imperialist nationalism, which makes it doubly difficult for women to challenge the dominant rugby discourse. Rugby constitutes a bastion of indigenous masculinity as a modern embodiment of Fijian warrior heritage, where transgression is equated with disrespect for indigenous tradition (Kanemasu and Molnar, 2017).

Consequently, women rugby players have been met with widespread disapproval, ridicule and punishment for claiming the masculine sport and for their (real or suspected) gender and sexual nonconformity. Until recently, the women operated in isolation, largely outside of the formal rugby governing structure, which organises men's rugby through the national union, provincial unions, local clubs and school rugby. This means that, while male players mostly received consistent funding and institutional support from the FRU, women were for many years left on their own to finance/organise their activities with sporadic support.

The challenges they faced, especially until a few years ago, were far greater than a simple absence of support. Male (and some female) spectators routinely ridiculed them using sexist and homophobic comments. Some women players were beaten by family members, turned out of their homes and/or ostracised by their communities. Some left by choice, lest their gender expression, sexuality and/or dedication to the masculine game be found out or condemned. Many of these women were unemployed, shared accommodation and helped each other in making a living (Kanemasu and Molnar, 2013b, 2017).

The women's determination to continue playing is underpinned by multiple factors. First, the players invariably speak of their undiluted passion and love for the game. Second, the passion is also often linked to the physical and 'combative' nature of the game as a medium of their gender expression and sense of empowerment not easily found in other social spheres. Third, for many players, claiming rugby is a conscious act of counter-hegemony. Finally, rugby provides these non-conforming women with a critical space for solidarity, mutual support and refuge from societal oppression.

Thus, pursuing rugby is far more than a physical activity for many of these women (see Kanemasu, Johnson and Molnar, 2018). Such passion, struggles and aspirations are captured in a Fijiana player's recent personal reflections:

> Rugby is my everything. When I was nothing – I had no job, I had no support from my parents – it was only rugby and a group of friends in rugby. When I was out there with nothing, it was rugby that occupied me. It built me; it told me, 'You are not alone. You have something'.

The women have begun to make outstanding international successes in recent years, winning the Bowl at the 2013 Rugby World Cup Sevens. In 2016, they became the first Pacific island women's rugby team to compete in the Olympics, while the Fijiana 15-a-side team won the 2016 and 2018 Oceania Rugby Women's Championships. In 2018, they had a successful Australian tour with convincing wins over the Brumbies and the Newcastle Hunters. These achievements, and especially the Fijiana sevens side's Olympic status, have had a considerable positive impact. The FRU today finances and organises national team selections, training camps and tours and promotes the sport among schoolgirls. Progress has also been made in integrating grass-roots women players into formal rugby governing and support mechanisms. In 2018, the FRU began mainstreaming women's games in provincial-level competitions (which had previously excluded women) and made it mandatory for all provisional unions to enlist a women's team. Fijiana players have started appearing in television commercials and advertising posters for local businesses. In 2017, the Fijiana were named among the '70 Inspiring Pacific Women' by a key regional organisation, the Pacific Community (2017). A recent study found a broad-based and substantial rise in community perceptions of, and support for, women's rugby (Kanemasu and Johnson, 2019). These appear to have stimulated an increase in the player population since 2012, when World Rugby (2012) estimated just 270 senior players and 100 teen players, although no official statistics are currently available. While there were only four to five women's rugby clubs in Suva a few years ago, today there are reportedly 28 across the country.

Yet, their struggle is far from over. While institutional support has increased, there remains a disparity between the resources and support accessible to women's and men's rugby. Significant gaps remain in women's performance pathway (Fijianas have, to date, been selected directly from local clubs, which is only just beginning to change). Negative sanctions at grassroots levels also persist, with catcalls and jeers from male players and bystanders on training grounds. In our recent interviews, women players themselves noted the continuing stigma and hostility experienced in the communities despite the current improvement.

RWC: 'It'll be a dream come true'

Women's rugby in Fiji is thus a product of many years of struggle and hard-won victories. In this journey, qualifying for a World Cup, along with Olympic qualification, has been the women's paramount goal and hope. In 2016, shortly after the Fijiana sevens side's historic participation in the Olympics, the Fijiana fifteens team began their pursuit of 2017 Women's RWC qualification. Following a successful match against Papua New Guinea (PNG) in the Oceania Rugby Women's Championship in 2016, they proceeded to play Hong Kong and Japan in the Asian Rugby Women's Championship in Hong Kong, where the top two countries qualified for the Women's RWC.

Representing Fiji in any international game is a pinnacle of their playing career. In a society where rugby is held with such esteem and directly connected with the aspirations of a postcolonial people, 'donning the Fiji jersey', as typically phrased in Fiji, is regarded as an utmost honour with great responsibilities: 'It's everyone's dream here to don the national jumper, and it's an honour to represent the country. It gives us an opportunity to put Fiji on the world map'. But on a collective level, this RWC qualification attempt, along with the Olympic qualification, was nothing less than epoch-making from their standpoint, as expressed by a squad member before departing for Hong Kong:

> It's the ultimate, the epitome of playing rugby, to be able to go to a World Cup and, of course, the Olympics as well. To be part of the team and to make history – 'cause we'll be the first Fijiana fifteens team to be able to go to a Rugby World Cup. You know, that is just an amazing achievement.

Furthermore, this qualification attempt had broader, transformative potential: to qualify for a World Cup in the 15-a-side, full rugby union game would provide the women with cultural legitimacy. As explained by another squad member:

> It [RWC qualification]'ll mean a lot for women's rugby in Fiji. This is something that we could only dream of. For it to actually take place–it'll be a dream come true. It'll be easier for girls [after qualification]. Girls will have an option to play rugby rather than grow

up in a family where you are always told to play netball. Now that we have women competing in the World Series and in the Olympics and now trying for the World Cup fifteens – it's gonna be a boost for women's rugby.

Seremaia Bai, a former international rugby star and women's rugby supporter, was recruited as Head Coach shortly before the preparations started. His motivation for involvement was:

> about equality, for women to be treated with respect and integrity. This is something I want to contribute, to fight for these women. They deserve more; they deserve a fair chance; they deserve opportunities, just like men ... That's my biggest motivation [for coaching the team]. Just to give them a chance.

Thus, the qualification attempt was an integral part of the women's counter-hegemonic struggle, which presented real transformative potential that excited the squad members and the entire women's rugby community. Maguire and Tuck (2005, p. 92) have described international sports as a form of 'patriot games', where athletes 'become highly visible embodiments of these nations ... [They] are significant actors who both define and reflect the "special charisma" of nations writ large'. RWC qualification was a battleground for the women players to decisively and publicly claim ownership of the most prestigious and culturally sanctioned masculine sport.

The Fijiana had a taste of this counter-hegemony during their game against PNG, which was their first 15-a-side international match in their home ground. There, one of us witnessed, for the first time, overwhelming spectator support for the Fijiana. The crowd loudly cheered for the team and screamed 'Go Fiji!'. The simple act of calling out 'Go Fiji!' is of enormous significance, as it endorses the women's legitimacy as rugby players and uncouples the discourses of national pride and masculinism. Perhaps, the most evocative moment was when the women performed *cibi*, the traditional war dance, conventionally staged by men's national teams prior to international matches. Fijian rugby players are 'modern warriors' who personify the unique martial tradition of their society. For women to perform this symbolic act loaded with nationalist and traditionalist sentiments was a remarkable milestone in their quest for appropriating the hegemonic rugby discourse:

> Ah, that was so exciting. I have been playing sevens all over the world; I hadn't played here in the national stadium. That feeling

is just overwhelming. When we had the national anthem, when we got to do the *cibi*, it just brought in a different spirit. You just wanna give it your all there on the field.

The squad left for Hong Kong in 2016 with great anticipation and pride, but within a week of their arrival, they played two matches against Japan and Hong Kong and lost them both.

Local-global double hurdle: gender and geopolitical relations of power

Our discussions have so far focused on the Fijiana's RWC qualification attempt in the context of gender and sexual politics of Fijian society. But their attempt was also profoundly shaped by broader power relations: in particular, North-South politico-economic disparity. This has long been a challenge faced by Fiji's men's rugby team (Kanemasu and Molnar, 2013a, 2014), but women players experience it as double marginalisation. While Fiji is severely disadvantaged in terms of material resources and political power in international rugby, women are further disadvantaged within Fiji rugby.

In examining the men's RWC, Harris and Wise (2011, p. 378) highlight a 'global divide between the eight foundation unions of the IRB and the rest of the rugby world'. Wise (2017) shows that while World Rugby has 100 member unions and 17 associate member unions, only 25 countries have ever competed in the RWC, with automatic qualifiers dominated by the eight 'core rugby playing nations'. In addition, although Asia and Oceania are deemed two different regions geographically, they were until recently treated as one region in qualification. Hence, for countries outside of the rugby core, competing for a place in the RWC entails jumping a structural hurdle which is further compounded by myriad economic hurdles in the case of global South nations. A parallel is seen in the Women's RWC. Seven out of the 12 competing countries in the 2017 Women's RWC were automatic qualifiers. In Oceania, New Zealand and Australia automatically qualified, which left Fiji, as third in the region after defeating PNG, to proceed to the repêchage competing with Hong Kong and Japan for the two places in the Asia/Oceania qualification. While both Japan and Hong Kong would be classified as peripheral in the rugby world system, they are global North nations in politico-economic terms. Consequently, the Fijiana fought for a place in the RWC against not only structural but considerable financial and infrastructural hurdles.

Japan and Hong Kong work on a four-year plan to prepare their women's teams for RWCs and other key competitions. A brief look at the resources and support available to women players in Hong Kong is helpful in contextualising the Fijiana's local-global double hurdle. Hong Kong has more than 4,500 registered female players, about a third of all registered rugby players (World Rugby, 2018). There is a professional rugby sevens programme for both men and women, whereby players are provided with full-time training programmes and contracts based at the Hong Kong Institute of Sport. Qualifying for the 2017 Women's RWC was one of 38 key projects in the 2016–2019 Hong Kong Rugby Union Strategic Plan. To this end, they developed a systematic performance pathway, where all national players, including professional sevens players, participated in an internal representative competition, which selected the best 66 players who competed against each other throughout the year (Hong Kong Rugby Union, 2019).

Rugby in Fiji, as in other Pacific island countries, currently does not have a professional structure due to limited broadcast/gate revenues owing to the lack of disposable income of local populations. Comparing their situation with Hong Kong, a Fijiana official stated:

> We are so far behind. [Hong Kong national players] are all paid by the government to play rugby ... Here, we have just a bunch of girls who got together. Half of them are not working. [Hong Kong players] have their own facilities, training ground, WiFi, ice machines and all that.

The Fijiana had about a month after the team selection to prepare for the qualifiers, with the coaching team appointed shortly prior to that. The preparation was riddled with challenges. The team hired a university dormitory for their camp to minimise expenses. In the absence of a team manager, the FRU Women's Rugby Development Officer temporarily took up the role. A team official's reflections are illustrative of the realities of the economics of World Cup competition:

> We didn't have a doctor. We didn't have someone to check their food every day. We only had [the Women's Rugby Development Officer] as a manager. They [Hong Kong and Japan] have a manager, assistant manager, a logistics manager; they have someone for everything, from booking the grounds to taking clothes to a laundry. It's money. Everything is money.

A telling example of the complexities of the socio-economic challenges faced by the team is nutritional management. Without specialist background, the temporary manager had to plan the team's daily menu and arrange catering within a limited budget. It was a formidable task to procure appropriate meals from affordable vendors who had no experience of catering for athletes. Moreover, provision of the right food at low cost was far from the only concern, as a team official explained:

> It's not easy. We have players who come from homes where they don't have money to buy healthy food. Healthy food here is very expensive. So they just eat whatever comes on the table. They were not used to eating balanced food.

Notably, while men's rugby in Fiji may not have access to the resources and structures that support their New Zealand or England counterparts, they take the primary share of what does exist in Fiji:

> You cannot prepare for a World Cup qualifier in one month. [Fijian] Men don't do that; they take four years to prepare for the next World Cup. Men have matches every year and a budget comes with it ... With the men, there is a pathway. They go from clubs to provincial [unions] to national [team]. With the women, from here [local clubs] to the national. There's a big gap; they [women] haven't been exposed to the professional set-up, the right food, the right training.

Despite glaring resource shortages, the FRU makes high-priority efforts to support men's RWC attempts to ensure continuity. The men's 2015 RWC pursuit was financially supported by statutory bodies, private businesses and the general public. The whole nation, even with limited resources, pulls together to support the men's RWC attempts. Consequently, the prevailing notion is: 'we need to focus on the men first ... Why bring in women when we have so much to deal with?'

Thus, the women are faced with local and global relations of power that doubly marginalise them. Many women players are acutely aware of this:

> I've noticed about the ones [players] overseas; they're either in school or they have very nice jobs ... The ones in Fiji ... don't finish high school, they don't finish tertiary ... That is the life that some of the rugby girls in Fiji live. It's something that is not known. I would say the ones overseas are very, very, very fortunate. I was looking at photos of some of the girls in [an Australian women's

rugby club]. They're so fortunate. The ones in Fiji don't have that kind of privileges, you know, because of playing rugby [as women] and the fact of being gay.

The lack of material and political resources means that women players absorb the deficit themselves. Women sacrifice employment/education to devote time to rugby in the absence of readily accessible player development support. They bear the financial and practical cost of organising their own games to compensate for the absence of a consistent game schedule (although this may be improved by the FRU's recent mainstreaming of women's games). They bear the physical and financial cost of injury incurred outside of national team duties. They continue to suffer the emotional cost of stigmatisation and abuse, in the absence of family/community support. In our previous study on men's rugby in Fiji, we highlighted that individual athletes, families and communities together 'pick up the tab' of player development and retirement in the absence of formal support (Kanemasu and Molnar, 2014). Male players make material and physical sacrifices with the hope of one day securing a professional contract overseas. Yet, they are sustained by their immediate or extended families. For women, professional prospects are currently virtually non-existent. As one player noted 'The cultural mind-set here is … men can make a career out of rugby [with overseas club contracts] but not women. So why support the women?'. Consequently, women players stand on their own, without the kind of family/community support men can rely on. They absorb the material, physical and emotional cost of global South rugby, with little to no likelihood of seeing any financial returns for their sacrifice.

Against all odds: quest for 'zero to hero'

The Fijiana lost to Hong Kong and Japan but a sense of fulfilment also emerged among the squad members as they departed. Competing in the RWC qualifiers was deeply satisfying for many on a personal level, and furthermore, their qualification attempt had claimed tentative victories. Many saw the PNG match as an achievement. While women's games normally have sparse public attention or occur during less popular time slots, the PNG game, the first international match in the fifteens game that presented the women as a national team at the prestigious national stadium, attracted a significant number of spectators showing enthusiastic support. For some, this was also the first time their family showed support: 'My brothers and sisters came to watch. I was really proud. I knew that I just made the change there, a voice to the community'.

In other words, the struggle between the hegemonic rugby discourse and a counter-hegemonic, emergent rugby discourse may be nearing a tipping point. (Counter-)hegemony is a strategic process of 'cultural battles', whereby a social group strives to elicit the consent of others by establishing a 'common conception of the world' (Gramsci, 1971, pp. 348–349). The RWC attempt showed the women that their cultural battle was at a critical stage of tipping the balance of public perception in their favour. As aptly expressed by a squad member:

> People were shouting [at the PNG game] for women's rugby! We wanted people to sit up and take notice that yes, women's rugby is here ... That is what we wanted to do. And I think we achieved it with that game, playing in front of a home crowd ... There was this group of men [among the spectators]. I think they initially came just to see how it [women's game] was. After a while ... they were saying, 'Hey, these girls know what they are doing!' We followed game patterns; we followed the game plan, and of course we kept that Fijian flair that we are known for!

In the Head Coach's view: 'I don't count successes by winning games. I see real success as making a change and impacting on people's lives'. The qualifier attempt was a success in advancing the women's battle to reconfigure the rugby discourse. Another squad member's comment just before the qualifier games epitomises this tenacity for effecting change:

> It [RWC qualification] is a huge challenge ... It's really big. But then, deep within me, it's a small thing to tackle, because we are born to be rugby players here in Fiji. Going out there, we wanna make a change, not only in Hong Kong but here in Fiji. We wanna make women's rugby run for life. We wanna put our stamp. We will make it work – we will *have to* make it work and make the nation proud [participant emphasis].

The 2017 RWC qualification attempt was a consequential moment in the women's quest to achieve 'zero to hero'. With the current trends of incremental changes in the dominant rugby discourse, increase in institutional support and continuing rise in the Fijiana's performance, there exists scope for them to score a major victory in tipping the scales. As a senior player summarised: 'We are on the verge of turning the corner. We're finally breaking through'.

Conclusion

This chapter outlined what it means to women players to claim the game against many adversities at personal/family/community/societal levels, and how RWC qualification holds out transformative potential to effect a critical shift in the hegemonic rugby discourse. We have also illuminated the multi-layered cost of rugby pursuit in Fiji as a global South society. The uneven playing-field becomes conspicuous in the race for the RWC due to the sheer politico-economic strain that the mega-event puts on competing nations. Fijian women players bear this cost largely on their own, without the support that their male counterparts have. The Fijiana's attempt to qualify for 2017 RWC hence took place against a backdrop of local-global double marginalisation. However, we have also argued that their attempt brought home to the women a vision of counter-hegemony and tangible signs that a substantive shift in the rugby discourse may indeed be achieved in the not so distant future. Such a counter-hegemonic victory would most likely entail transformative impact beyond the game, in the broader gender power dynamics in Fijian society. RWC qualification, therefore, remains a primary project with multiple possibilities and implications for these non-conforming women: '2021 will be our year. If we qualify, just once, that'll be our success story'.

Acknowledgements

We are deeply grateful to the 2016 Fijiana fifteens squad, Seremaia Bai, Ro Alifereti Doviverata, Vela Naucukidi and other team officials who allowed Yoko to visit their RWC preparation camp. Any errors found in this chapter are solely ours and should not be attributed to any of these individuals.

References

Cattermole, J. (2008). We are Fiji: Rugby, music and the representation of the Fijian nation. *Shima: The International Journal of Research into Island Cultures*, 2, 99–115.

Fiji Rugby Union (2019). About us. *Fiji Rugby Union*, 13 January. www.fijirugby.com/rugby-house/about-us/

Fiji Women's Crisis Centre (2013). *Somebody's life, everybody's business! National research on women's health and life experiences in Fiji (2010/2011): A survey exploring the prevalence, incidence and attitudes to intimate partner violence in Fiji*. Suva: Fiji Women's Crisis Centre.

Gramsci, A. (1971). *Selections from the prison notebooks* (ed. and trans. Q Hoare and G.N. Smith). New York: International Publishers.

Guinness, D., and Besnier, N. (2016). Nation, nationalism, and sport: Fijian rugby in the local–global nexus. *Anthropological Quarterly*, 89(4), 1109–1141.

Harris, J., and Wise, N. (2011). Geographies of scale in international rugby union. *Geographical Research*, 49(4), 375–383.

Hong Kong Rugby Union (2019). Women's national 15s. *Hong Kong Rugby Union*, 1 February. www.hkrugby.com/national/national-team/womens-national-15s

Kanemasu, Y., and Johnson, J. (2019). Exploring the complexities of community attitudes towards women's rugby: Multiplicity, continuity and change in Fiji's hegemonic rugby discourse. *International Review for the Sociology of Sport*, 54(1), 86–103.

Kanemasu, Y., Johnson, J., and Molnar, G. (2018). Fiji's women rugby players: Finding motivation in a 'hostile' environment. In G. Molnar, S. Amin and Y. Kanemasu (Eds.) *Women, sport and exercise in the Asia-Pacific region: Domination-resistance-accommodation*. London: Routledge (pp. 141–158).

Kanemasu, Y., and Molnar, G. (2013a). Pride of the people: Fijian rugby labour migration and collective identity. *International Review for the Sociology of Sport*, 48(6), 720–735.

Kanemasu, Y., and Molnar, G. (2013b). Problematising the dominant: The emergence of alternative cultural voices in Fiji rugby. *Asia Pacific Journal of Sport and Social Science*, 2(1), 14–30.

Kanemasu, Y., and Molnar, G. (2014). Life after rugby: Issues of being an 'ex' in Fiji rugby. *International Journal of the History of Sport*, 31(11), 1389–1405.

Kanemasu, Y., and Molnar, G. (2017). Double-trouble: Negotiating gender and sexuality in post-colonial women's rugby in Fiji. *International Review for the Sociology of Sport*, 52(4), 430–446.

Maguire, J., and Tuck, J. (2005). National identity, rugby union and notions of Ireland and the 'Irish'. *Irish Journal of Sociology*, 14(1), 86–109.

Pacific Community (2017). Fijiana rugby team. *Pacific Community*, 3 October. www.spc.int/70-inspiring-pacific-women/fijiana-rugby-team/

Presterudstuen, G. (2010). The mimicry of men: Rugby and masculinities in post-colonial Fiji. *The Global Studies Journal*, 3(2), 237–247.

Ramsay, G. (2018). Rugby World Cup: In a world of organized sport, Fiji bucks the trend. *CNN*, 8 February 2019. https://edition.cnn.com/2018/12/18/sport/rugby-fiji-flying-fijians-john-mckee-ben-ryan-world-cup-japan-spt-intl/index.html

Wise, N. (2017). Rugby World Cup: New directions or more of the same? *Sport in Society*, 20(3), 341–354.

World Economic Forum (2018). The global gender gap report. Cologny/Geneva, Switzerland. *World Economic Forum*, 11 January 2019. www3.weforum.org/docs/WEF_GGGR_2018.pdf

World Rugby (2012). Fiji. *World Rugby*, 15 January 2013. www.irb.com/unions/union.11000030/index.html

World Rugby (2018). Conference lays foundations for continued growth in Hong Kong. *World Rugby*, 2 February 2019. www.world.rugby/news/363949

4 From past to present
Is there room for professional rugby in the United States of America?

Lindsey Gaston and Lara Killick

Introduction

The year 2018 was a big year for rugby union in the world's largest sports market, the USA. The Men's Eagles secured their first Tier 1 victory in 94 years, with a win over sixth ranked Scotland, moving them to 12th in the world rankings. While the Women's Eagles cemented their fifth place world ranking and made history with the first ever all-women broadcast team in rugby during an international game in the US. In rugby sevens, the men won their first series gold medal with 28-0 victory against Argentina in Las Vegas and subsequently reached Number 1 in the HSBC World Rugby Sevens Standings for the first time. Year 2018 also marked the first time a Rugby World Cup was held on American soil. In July, San Francisco hosted the seventh men's, and third women's, Rugby World Cup Sevens tournament. The event reported record-breaking US attendance and TV viewership figures with 8.7 million unique viewers tuning in to watch the 24 men's and 16 women's teams compete for victory (USA Rugby, 2019). However, despite these recent achievements on the international stage, rugby remains a peripheral sport in the US professional sport landscape and the US remains a peripheral rugby nation in an international context, albeit one with immense potential.

It is this potential that operates as the focus of this chapter and prompts the question: does the USA have the market capacity and cultural space for professional rugby? Drawing on historical data, this chapter presents the reputable history of US rugby within amateur and collegiate settings before exploring growing participation rates, attendance trends at international matches and US consumer interest in the sport. The second half of this chapter explores contemporary efforts to introduce professional men's rugby in the USA. We conclude by examining the potential sustainability of these strategic plans and professional rugby in the USA more broadly.

History of rugby in the USA

Rugby is not a new import to the pantheon of US sport. The origin of rugby in the USA can be traced back to the elite institutions of higher education (Park, 1984). Steeped in the reputation and Muscular Christianity ethos of the English Public Schools, rugby promoted the leadership qualities, teamwork, discipline and respect desired by the academic male elite in nineteenth-century America (Dunning and Sheard, 1979). Indeed, it is the prevalent belief that the first rugby match on US soil occurred in 1874 between Harvard University and McGill University (PFRA Research, 2019). That match would provide the foundation for the creation of the Intercollegiate Football Association (IFA) in 1876 by Columbia, Harvard, Princeton and Yale Universities to formalise the sport by officially adopting the traditional rules of rugby union. The IFA was the first of its kind in the US and would eventually underpin the group of elite institutions commonly known as the Ivy League.

Throughout the early 1900s, the game experienced a steady growth in popularity fuelled by a popular campaign espousing the dangers of American Football (Richards, 2013; Ryan, 2004); in 1905, 18 amateur athletes died while competing in collegiate football games (Watterson, 2000). As a result, several universities (including Columbia, Northwestern and Duke) banned American Football. Advocates positioned rugby as the safer, more civilised version of the two games. Amidst fears surrounding the 'violent play, serious injuries and evidence of sharp practice by college [American Football] coaches', interest and participation in rugby at the college level increased (Richards, 2013). Two notable universities (Stanford and the University of California Berkeley) switched codes as rugby replaced American Football in their athletic schedules from 1906 to 1917. The surge in rugby's popularity peaked with New Zealand's historic 1913 tour of Northern California, Nevada and Canada. As only the second time the All Blacks had toured outside of Australasia, the 1913 visit increased the game's profile among American spectators. However, the performance gap evident between the New Zealand national side and their various US opponents also reminded the host nation of their relative youth and inexperience in the game. Indeed, many commentators at the time linked these defeats to colleges' decision to return to American Football and a reduction in rugby participation in the region (Richards, 2013). The subsequent gold medal successes of the USA rugby team at the 1920 and 1924 Olympic Games did little to stem the decline of the game within collegiate sport.

However, the 1960s and 1970s was a time of renaissance for rugby in the United States (Freeman, 2018; Pritchett, 2018). Similar to the sport's origins in the US, American Universities would play a significant role. In 1961, the US Military Academy established the USA Army Rugby Club, with other military academies swiftly following suit. The resurgence of rugby in these military institutions encouraged America's Northern neighbour, Canada, to re-establish the Canadian Rugby Union in 1965 (Rugby Canada, 2019). Rugby started to gain greater traction across university campuses in the US, specifically on the west coast where the weather and access to grass fields facilitated the growth of the game. Rugby remains relatively popular within universities and colleges across the nation with university rugby membership now accounting for a third of USA Rugby's membership (Rugby Business Executive Association, 2018). While the game is consistently recognised as one the fast-growing and popular sports within the university setting in the USA (Pritchett, 2018; Swenson, 2018; This is American Rugby, 2014), rugby is not among the 24 National Collegiate Athletics Association (NCAA) sanctioned sports. Instead, USA Rugby retains governance oversight of men's and women's university rugby. In men's rugby, three levels of competitive leagues are offered, Division II, Division IAA and the Elite Division 1A competition. Since 2011, 72 men's college rugby teams across eight conferences have participated in the Division 1A competition with Life University defeating the perennial powerhouse University of California, Berkeley, to claim the 2018 title.

Similarly, three levels of competitive leagues exist in women's university rugby, Division II, Division I and the Elite Division 1 competitions. Unlike its male counterpart, women's rugby was classified as an NCAA Emerging Sport in 2002 enabling schools to count participation towards their Title IX mandates. While the history of women's rugby in the USA is a shorter tale, the amount of success they have amassed in less than 50 years is impressive. The establishment of women's rugby occurred at the same time the sport was experiencing a renewed focus among university students and was assisted by the introduction of Title IX, a ground-breaking piece of gender equity education legislation. In 1972, the year of Title IX's implementation, the first three documented female rugby teams were established at Colorado State University, University of Colorado and the University of Illinois. Over the decade, more female teams would organise and add to the wave of female participation in rugby. The 1980s were significant for the women's game, with the creation of the first US Women's National Team (USWNT) in 1985. This group of pioneering women would lead an undefeated tour through France and England (Womensrugbyhistory, 1985). Two years later, USA Women's Rugby would officially be recognised by USA Rugby, earning the moniker the 'Women's Eagles'. With their newly granted wings, USA Women's rugby rose quickly in the international game. The Women's Eagles became the inaugural Women's Rugby World Champions in 1991 and successfully reclaimed their title in 1994 and 1998. As of February 2019, USWNT rank fifth globally, seven places higher than their male counterparts. This ranking is even more impressive when noting the fact that the women's squad did not have a full-time Head Coach until 2018.

Contemporary participation and consumer interest in rugby

However, it would be naive to suggest that the participation in rugby is warehoused among the university club teams and interest reserved solely for university students. Rugby is also recognised as one of the fastest growing sports outside of the university structure (Soleimani, 2018). From a participation perspective, interest in the game is growing. Rugby's profile received a significant boost in the US after the International Olympic Committee's announcement in 2009 that rugby would return to the 2016 Olympic Games. Data suggests that rugby participation in the US has 'risen 43% since 2010, a fact accentuated by its inclusion in the Olympics' (Swenson, 2018). This growth is concentrated among the 18- to 24-year-old demographic, with an 11.2% increase among men and a 12.2% increase among women. According to USA Rugby's Operational Strategy for 2020, 117,129 people are registered members of the governing body (USA Rugby, 2018). The distribution of registered members across the various categories is presented in Table 4.1.

Table 4.1 USA Rugby membership in 2018

Category	Membership
Club	29,073 (26.7%)
College/U20	34,004 (29%)
High school	30,862 (26.3%)
Youth/Rookie	15,020 (12.8%)
Coaches, referees and/or administration	8,180 (7%)

Further examination shows that the highest concentration of membership occurs along the west coast and in the New England and Rocky Mountain regions in the US (Rugby Business Executive Association, 2018). These areas of membership concentration correspond with previous attempts to establish a professional league.

In terms of spectators, there has been a steady growth in event attendance and TV viewership within the country. In a 2009 exhibition match between the USA and Ireland, 10,000 fans were in attendance (ESPN, 2018). Three years later, over 17,000 people watched USA take on Italy in Houston, Texas (This is American Rugby, 2014). Subsequent games against Ireland in 2013 and Scotland in 2014 both boasted crowds of over 20,000. However, all previous attendance numbers paled in comparison when the leading global (national rugby) brand, the New Zealand All Blacks, played the Men's Eagles in 2014. A crowd of 61,500 spectators attended the game at Soldier Field in Chicago, Illinois, and an additional 927,000 watching on television (ESPN, 2018). American interest in rugby has also been supported by the continued growth in the attendance of USA Rugby Sevens tournament hosted in Las Vegas, Nevada. Attendance grew considerably from 15,800 people in 2004 to 52,000 people in 2012 (Goff, 2018). By 2017, over 80,000 people attended the three-day competition. From 2004 to 2017, rugby sevens has experienced a significant increase in event attendance.

This explosion in event attendance may be explained by several interconnecting factors. In the first instance, the fast pace style of play associated with the sevens format may be more attractive to US audiences than its 15-a-side counterpart. An easier version of the game for novice audiences to consume, rugby sevens is dynamic, free-flowing and often high scoring. The reduced playing time (7- to 10-minute halves versus 40-minute halves in 15-a-side rugby) appeals to shorter attention spans and provides opportunities for commercial breaks and media 'timeouts', which is common in US sports. Furthermore, the inclusion of rugby sevens in the 2016 Olympics, the recent success of US Men's sevens team, and the existence of recognisable US athletes such as Perry Baker and Carlin Isles in the global game have each helped raise the visibility of rugby within the congested US sports market. Yet, amidst this growth, the men's professional game has struggled to establish a consistent presence in the market. Attempts to launch a professional league have encountered a host of structural and logistical challenges, to which this chapter now turns.

The development of men's professional rugby in the US

Since the dawn of the professional era in 1995, the US Men's elite XV competition structure has undergone multiple iterations, moving from the long-standing amateur USA Rugby Super League (1995–2012) to its current professional format, Major League Rugby (MLR; 2018–present).

Despite experiencing a myriad of challenges, the amateur Super League maintained its presence as the top tier domestic competition for 16 years. Initially, the Super League operated as an independent sports organisation akin to the National Basketball Association (NBA) or National Football League (NFL; ESPN, 2000). The private company delivered a single league 'closed competition' devoid of the promotion/relegation paths found in other countries. While unusual in traditional rugby-playing nations, such closed competitions are common across many professional sports in the US (e.g. baseball, soccer, basketball and American football). The Super League's opening season contained 14 teams, split into two geographical divisions (Midwestern-East and Western-Pacific). The Gentlemen of Aspen were crowned inaugural champions following their 22-8 defeat of Old Blue. Season 2 saw the competition expand to 16 teams with two new teams joining Midwestern-East and one established team transferring to Western-Pacific. This structure remained stable until 2000 when, as part of a broader restructuring of player performance pathways, USA Rugby subsumed the competition into its operations and took administrative and commercial responsibility for the Super League. In its new position as a USA Rugby sanctioned competition, the Super League now featured promotion/relegation and was the cornerstone of the elite performance pathway. In 2002, the geographical divisions were dissolved in an attempt to mirror the domestic league structures more commonly found in other rugby-playing nations. The logistics of managing the geographically large market meant this experiment was short-lived and the competition returned to its original format in 2005. However, fluctuating team membership, insufficient funding and low sponsor interest ultimately led to Super League's demise in 2012.

It's replacement, the smaller USA Rugby Elite Cup lasted just a single season. Beset by similar challenges as its forbearer, journalists speculated that the Elite Cup could not overcome the political infighting between the eight Elite Cup teams and USA Rugby (Willoughby, 2014). The emergence of amateur regional premiership competitions sealed the Elite Cup's fate as three of the eight Elite Cup teams defected to the new, non-USA Rugby sanctioned Pacific Rugby Premiership (PRP) at the close of the 2013 season. Over the following three years, two additional regional competitions emerged: the American Rugby Premiership (2014) and Midwest Rugby Premiership (2015). Across these three premierships, 21 amateur clubs continue to play in structured regional competitions throughout the traditional Northern Hemisphere season. The MWRP also compete in the annual USA Rugby-sponsored Gold Cup, a crossover event with the Red River Division 1A conference.

The combined failures of the Super League and Elite Cup did not deter USA Rugby from its strategic goal of establishing a viable professional league for men's rugby. In 2015, they announced the launch of the Professional Rugby Organization (PRO) in partnership with World Rugby (USA Rugby, 2015). The first fully professional format of rugby in the US, PRO Rugby provided financial stability for US national players, the opportunity to train year-round and compete against one another in an elite domestic competition. Previously, members of the US men's national team were required to migrate overseas in order to obtain such benefits. For example, Chris Wyles, who won 54 caps for the USA, played for Saracens in the English premiership. Over his ten-year career with Saracens, he appeared 252 times, scored 74 tries and won four premiership titles and two European champion titles.

Five teams participated in the inaugural 2016 season with the Denver Stampede emerging champions by securing a bonus point in their away defeat against Ohio Aviators (Bechtel, 2016). However, 2016 was to be the first and only season of PRO Rugby. The off-season period revealed substantial organisational problems and strategic failures. Multiple PRO Rugby employees, including Steve Lewis (Director of Rugby) and Paul Keeler (West Coast Director of Operations) filed grievances with USA Rugby and pursued restitution through the courts for unpaid salaries and other expenses (Clifton, 2016a). Numerous players, coaches and other vendors also reported delayed payment, contract violations regarding healthcare provision and poor working conditions (Clifton, 2016a). Financed almost exclusively by a single investor, their CEO Doug Schoninger, PRO proved fiscally unsound. A breakdown in contract negotiations between PRO Rugby and Rugby Canada regarding the former obtaining exclusive operating rights north of the border stalled expansion plans and further compounded PRO Rugby's financial struggles (Blum, 2016).

Eight months after its opening game, PRO Rugby terminated player contracts citing 'serious issues with the cooperation and enforcement of our agreement with USA Rugby' (Clifton, 2016b). Schoninger alleged that USA Rugby violated their agreement by promoting a rival start-up, while PRO Rugby held the exclusive rights for professional rugby in the US (Fischer, 2018). USA Rugby denied all allegations and the acrimonious relationship between the two organisations rumbles on. In June 2018, Doug Schoninger filed a lawsuit against USA Rugby, Rugby International Marketing and four USA Rugby representatives claiming the defendants 'engaged in extensive tortious misconduct and contractual breaches' (N.A Rugby Union LLC v USA Rugby Union, 2018). At the time of writing, the case remains open.

Meanwhile the rival start-up at the centre of the dispute, MLR formally launched its professional operations in November 2017 without an official USA Rugby sanction (Clifton, 2017). A single-entity league modelled after Major League Soccer (MLS), MLR is owned by its member clubs, each of which is privately owned. In this regard, it appears as though the MLR powerbrokers have learned an important lesson from the monopolistic ownership of PRO Rugby. The league's inaugural season opened in April 2018 with seven teams competing for the championship title. After a successful first season, the league added two expansion teams in 2019 and replaced PRO Rugby as the USA Rugby sanctioned professional rugby product. The size of the league continues to grow, with MLR confirming plans to incorporate two additional teams in 2020, bringing total membership to 11.

MLR has also been relatively successful in attracting quality international players nearing the end of their careers. For example, Ben Foden, a former England full back joined Rugby United New York for the 2019 season after a long career with Northampton Saints. Again, MLR appears to have learned from the experiences of other nascent professional leagues. Similar migration trends were noted in ice hockey (Elliott and Maguire, 2008) and basketball (Falcous and Maguire, 2005) leagues in Great Britain in the 1990s, where experienced players migrated from Canada and the US, respectively. Correspondingly, MLS adopted a Designated Player Rule in 2007 to attract global superstars (e.g. David Beckham) and raise the calibre of their on-field product (see Shapiro, DeSchriver and Rascher, 2017). The latter has certainly benefitted from this strategic approach. While still in its formative years, the MLR certainly appears a more stable operation than its predecessor. That said, the establishment of a professional sport is not easy and sustaining early growth opportunities is a difficult task.

Concluding thoughts

There are numerous challenges to the sustainability of professional men's rugby in the USA. Even when a sport is popular, the transition from an amateur to professional format can be difficult. In England, rugby's transition to professionalism revealed a lack of formal structures suitable for handling the changing demands of the game. The large level of corporate sponsorship expected was slow to occur and jeopardised the financial operations of the professional format (Gaston, 2014). Financial insecurity was compounded by a heavy reliance on revenue streams through untested ticket sales and in many cases, teams created unrealistic business plans that bled into every facet of their operational performance including, but not limited to, the employment rights and welfare needs of the new professional player (Gaston, 2014). However, the clubs' deep historical roots in their local communities and international recognition as the birthplace of the modern game enabled some of the professional clubs to attract international investment helping with the financial underwriting of professional club rugby. This resulted in the English national team developing a level of brand equity and added value regarding their professional rugby product.

Exposure, time and emotional connections are vital components in the creation of brand value (Aaker, 1991; Blackston, 1992; Keller, 1993). Due to PRO Rugby's short lifespan and the relative youth of the MLR format, the level of competitive ability is still being established for consumption. Similarly, there are limited stories of professional rugby success and few domestic players or coaches with iconic status. As a result, fan identification is relatively low as there has not been enough time to build a new consumer market. In light of the importance of emotional connections in building brand equity, both PRO Rugby and MLR established teams in parts of the country with a high concentration of identified rugby interest. Three of the five PRO Rugby teams were located in California, a state with high USA Rugby Membership. A fourth team was located in Denver, Colorado, a city with one of the highest USA Rugby memberships per capita. Similarly, 50% of the MLR teams are either located in states that have the highest absolute number of USA Rugby memberships (e.g. California and New York) or areas that have the densest USA Rugby membership per capita rates (e.g. Colorado and Utah).

Professional rugby in the USA not only has to create brand value for the sport, they must compete against an already crowded North American sports market. With an estimated value of $519.9 billion in 2017, the US sports industry is the largest in the world (Plunkett Analytics, 2018). Major professional leagues and teams operating within the US command a market of approximately $37.4 billion (Plunkett Analytics, 2018). The commercial US sports enterprise is dominated by the NFL, a sport that shares several similarities with rugby. Both full contact sports, American football and rugby, involve intense physical activity, punishing tackles and compete in hypermasculine cultural spaces (Pringle, 2001). Mirroring the 'football crisis' of 1906, current concerns related to the long-term health risks associated with American Football participation may open a window for rugby to draw some of the NFL's fan base and younger players towards their alternative product (see Maroon et al., 2015). Indeed, USA Rugby has already begun to mine the talent pool created by high school athletes who do not transition into a college career and/or collegiate athletes who do not 'go pro'. Of specific interest are those athletes with transferable skills from sports such as football or track and field (Tabani, 2019). However, with recent sports medicine research indicating that elite rugby may carry similar long-term health risks to football, this strategic approach may be limited in its appeal (see Gardner et al., 2014). Chapter 9 will outline some of the key challenges facing rugby in relation to the health and well-being of players.

Finally, some well-established men's rugby competitions from other nations have begun forays into the US market. For example, in 2016, Premiership Rugby (England) committed to hosting one regular season premiership game per year in the USA. The organisation has also established several strategic partnerships with US corporate entities in attempts to expand their global market presence. Most recently, the 2018/2019 season title sponsorship was sold to Arthur J Gallagher & Co, a large US insurance company. Similarly, Pro 14 has made its global intentions clear and wishes to establish a 'permanent foothold' in the US market with the inclusion of a team on the east coast (Lowe, 2017). Such expansion efforts represent both a challenge and opportunity to the burgeoning domestic professional structure in the USA. They represent competition for the limited media, economic and cultural capital available. There is the possibility that Premiership Rugby might be able to trade on their well-established brand equity, visibility and mobilise their cadre of iconic players and coaches to attract fans and corporate investment. Conversely, the entrance of mature brands could serve to increase interest in rugby, which may translate to an increase in the attention paid to US Rugby and its affiliate products. This 'rising tide, lifts all boats' approach is yet to be substantiated by industry data.

References

Aaker, D. (1991). *Managing brand equity: Capitalizing on the value of a brand name*. New York: Jossey Bass.
Bechtel, N. (2016). Ohio Aviators come up short of championship in final weekend. Available at www.nbc4i.com/news/ohio-aviators-come-up-short-of-championship-in-final-weekend/1114602324
Blackston, M. (1992). Observations: Building brand equity by managing the brand's relationships. *Journal of Advertising Research*, 32(3), 79–83.
Blum, B. (2016). U.S league doesn't want Canadian players. *CBC Sports*, Available at www.cbc.ca/sports/pro-rugby-elusive-canada-1.3845019
Clifton, P. (2016a). Pro's outstanding bills at the forefront of USA Rugby row. *Rugby Today*, Available at www.rugbytoday.com/elite/pros-outstanding-bills-forefront-usa-rugby-row
Clifton, P. (2016b). Down goes PRO. *Rugby Today*, Available at www.rugbytoday.com/elite/down-goes-pro
Clifton, P. (2017). Major League Rugby to launch with 9 teams. *Rugby Today*, Available at www.rugbytoday.com/clubs/major-league-rugby-launch-9-teams
Dunning, E., and Sheard, K. (1979). *Barbarians, gentleman & players: A sociological study of the development of rugby football*. New York: New York University Press.
Elliott, R., and Maguire, J. (2008). 'Getting caught in the net': Examining the recruitment of Canadian players in British professional ice hockey. *Journal of Sport and Social Issues*, 32(2), 158–176.
ESPN (2000). Super League sanctioned by USA Rugby. Available at www.espn.com/rugby/story/_/id/15346883/super-league-sanctioned-usa-rugby
ESPN (2018). Rugby Union, United States of America, highest attendance. *ESPN Scrum*, Available at http://stats.espnscrum.com/scrum/rugby/records/team/highest_attendance.html?id=11;type=team
Falcous, M., and Maguire, J. (2005). Globetrotters and local heroes? Labor migration, basketball, and local identities. *Sociology of Sport Journal*, 22(2), 137–157.
Fischer, B. (2018). USA Rugby now being sued by founder of now-defunct PRO Rugby League. *Sports Business Daily*, Available at www.sportsbusinessdaily.com/Daily/Issues/2018/06/06/Leagues-and-Governing-Bodies/Rugby.aspx
Freeman, A. (2018). The Beginning of 7s in the US. *Rugby Today*, Available at www.rugbytoday.com/historical/beginning-7s-us
Gaston, L. (2014). The rugby players association's benevolent fund: A sociological study of the development of a social integration discourse in rugby football (Doctoral dissertation, Durham University).
Gardner, A.., Iverson, G., Williams, W., Baker, S., and Stanwell, P. (2014). A systematic review and meta-analysis of concussion in rugby union. *Sports Medicine*, 44(12), 1717–1731.

Goff, A. (2018). Home. *Rugby Today*, Available at http://rugbymag.com/index.php?option=com_content&view=article&id=251:goffonrugby-the-big-deal&catid=96:goff-on-rugby&Itemid=292

Keller, K. (1993). Conceptualizing, measuring, and managing customer-based brand equity. *Journal of Marketing*, 57(1), 1–22.

Lowe, A. (2017). East-coast American side will join Pro14. *The Times*, Available at www.thetimes.co.uk/edition/sport/east-coast-american-side-will-join-pro14-qzh9tn7fm

Maroon, J., Winkelman, R., Bost, J., Amos, A., Mathyssek, C., and Miele, V. (2015). Chronic traumatic encephalopathy in contact sports: A systematic review of all reported pathological cases. *PLoS ONE*, 10(2), 1–16.

Park, R. (1984). From football to rugby – and back, 1906–1919: The University of California-Stanford University response to the 'football crisis of 1905'. *Journal of Sport History*, 11(3), 5–40.

PFRA Research (2019). No Christian end! The beginnings of football in America. Available at www.profootballresearchers.com/articles/No_Christian_End.pdf

Plunkett Analytics (2018). *Spectator Sports, Including Professional Sports Teams, Race Tracks and Motor Sports Revenues Market Size Forecasts Benchmarks Analysis*. Houston, TX: Plunkett Research Ltd.

Pritchett, J. (2018). Why pro rugby could win in the United States. *Forbes*, Available at www.forbes.com/sites/sportsmoney/2011/02/25/why-pro-rugby-could-win-in-the-united-states/#7a01a7f04636

Pringle, R. (2001). Competing discourses: Narratives of a fragmented self, manliness and rugby union. *International Review for the Sociology of Sport*, 36(4), 425–439.

Richards, H. (2013). The tour that killed American rugby. *ESPN scrum*, Available at http://en.espn.co.uk/newzealand/rugby/story/204045.html

Rugby Business Executive Association (2018). *Strategy 2020 Operational Objectives*. Available at www.rugbystrategy.us/

Rugby Canada (2019). History. Available at https://rugby.ca/en/about/history

Ryan, G. (2004). 'Brawn against brains': Australia, New Zealand and the American 'football crisis', 1906–13. *Sporting Traditions*, 20(2), 26.

Shapiro, S., DeSchriver, T., and Rascher, D. (2017). The Beckham effect: Examining the longitudinal impact of a star performer on league marketing, novelty, and scarcity. *European Sport Management Quarterly*, 17(5), 610–634.

Soleimani, S. (2018). What is the fastest growing sport in America? Available at https://blog.sisuguard.com/what-is-the-fastest-growing-sport-in-america

Swenson, M. (2018). Lacrosse and Rugby top fastest-growing sports. *Connect Sports*, Available at www.connectsports.com/feature/lacrosse-rugby-top-fastest-growing-sports/

Tabani, A. (2019). USA Rugby partners with 5 NGBs to launch Team USA pro days series. Available at www.usarugby.org/2019/04/usa-rugby-partners-with-five-ngbs-to-launch-team-usa-pro-days-series/

This is American Rugby (2014). American rugby must keep momentum going. Available at www.thisisamericanrugby.com/2014/11/american-rugby-must-keep-momentum-going.html

USA Rugby (2015). PRO Rugby launches first professional league in North America. Available at www.usarugby.org/2015/11/pro-rugby/

USA Rugby (2018). USA Rugby strategy. Available at www.rugbystrategy.us/

USA Rugby (2019). Rugby World Cup Sevens 2018 generates positive impact for San Francisco bay area. Available at www.usarugby.org/2018/12/rugby-world-cup-sevens-2018-generates-positive-impact-for-san-francisco-bay-area/

Watterson, J. (2000). The Gridiron crisis of 1905: Was it really a crisis? *Journal of Sport History*, 27(2), 291–298.

Willoughby, K. (2014). The fallout from the elite Cup demise: What next for D1 US Rugby? Available at https://lastwordonsports.com/2014/01/19/the-fallout-from-the-elite-cup-demise-what-next-for-d1-us-rugby/

Womensrugbyhistory (1985). American Barbarians tour of England. Available at http://womensrugbyhistory.blogspot.com/1985/11/times-nov-23-1985-pg.html

5 Struggling for recognition
Developing rugby union in Lebanon

Danyel Reiche and Axel Maugendre

Introduction

When thinking about rugby union and Lebanon, many fans of the sport might first think of Michael Cheika, Head Coach of the Australian national team, who is of Lebanese origin. What might be less known is that rugby union has also developed in Lebanon, although it is relatively new to the multi-religious West Asian country with a population of around six million people. The establishment of both men's and women's rugby union in the country was a response to external influences. In the case of men's rugby union, the British Embassy looked for a local Lebanese team to play against a British navy team in 1995. In the case of women's rugby union, an Egyptian women's team travelled to Lebanon in 2012 and searched for opponents. A key feature of rugby in Lebanon is that it is one of the few countries in which league is more popular than union, although recent successes in the recognition of the Lebanese Rugby Union Federation (LRUF) might give the sport a boost in the tiny Mediterranean country.

While there is a small but growing body of academic literature on Lebanese sports (e.g. Blanc, 2005; Mina, 2015; Nassif, 2013; Nassif and Amara 2015; Reiche, 2011), there is a lack of scholarly work on rugby union in the country. The only existing academic sources are an article by Reiche (2018) that focuses more on rugby league and a documentary by Enzo Baudino (2018) which features interviews with female and male Lebanese rugby union players. Apart from utilising these secondary sources, we collected primary data by conducting interviews with eight people between November 2018 and March 2019. Most were interviewed on more than one occasion. Interviewees included Nadim Abboud who invented scout rugby in Lebanon many years prior to rugby union's launch in the country; Abdallah Ali Jammal, chairman of the LRUF from its establishment in 2009 until 2018;

Mohammad Berro, who belongs like Jammal to the first generation of rugby union players in Lebanon; two players from the national women's team, Sarah Aouad and Douha Knio; Mazen Ramadan from the National Olympic Committee; and Steve Wrigglesworth, coach of the national men's team. Finally, information was obtained from Remond Safi from the Lebanese Rugby League Federation (LRLF) so that we could compare rugby union to rugby league in Lebanon.

The main purpose of the interviews was to acquire the respondents' knowledge and views on the historical development of rugby union in Lebanon.

Both authors have closely followed rugby union in Lebanon over many years: one of us (Axel Maugendre) is a rugby player and coach of the youth national men Under 18 team. Danyel Reiche is an academic in Lebanon and regularly interacts with officials and players in both codes of rugby. He has also published work on rugby league development in Lebanon (Reiche, 2018).

Establishing men's rugby union in Lebanon

In November 1995, when the British Embassy in Lebanon was preparing a brief stay in Beirut for HMS Cardiff, a ship of the Royal Navy (the United Kingdom's naval warfare force), it was also planning to organise a rugby union match for the ship's team. Embassy staff contacted Lebanese citizens who were exposed to rugby union when growing up abroad and asked them to form a team. Abdallah Ali Jammal was one of the players who founded the Beirut Phoenicians in October 1995. He lived in the South of England for 30 years and played rugby union in the 1970s for Worcester. He was part of the team that won the sevens and 15-a-side double North Midland Cup in 1978. For Jammal and other diaspora players who spent their childhoods abroad and later moved to Lebanon, playing rugby union made them feel back at home.

When interviewed for this research, Jammal remembered that the match against the crew of HMS Cardiff in November 1995 took place on the greenfield of the American University of Beirut (AUB), a leading university in Lebanon and the Arab world. The game, which was won by the navy team, even had the British ambassador in attendance. After the match and following only a few more days in Beirut, the ship left Lebanon, but the game marked the beginning of rugby union's young history in the country.

The Beirut Phoenicians continued to play matches against foreign soldiers in 1996. Mohammad Berro recalled that he played many games against Irish soldiers. Berro, who is known in the Lebanese rugby union community as 'Big Mo', was exposed to rugby union when he studied in France, a country with close ties to Lebanon. Lebanon was a French mandate from 1923 until 1946. There is one French university in the country, Saint Joseph University, and 43 schools recognised by Agency for French Education Abroad (AEFE), making Lebanon the second country behind the United States in terms of AEFE-recognised schools (AEFE, 2019). Studying in France is common among French-educated Lebanese students, and this experience has exposed some of the first cohort of rugby union players in Lebanon, such as Berro, to the sport. In 2009, Lebanon hosted the Francophone Games, although rugby was not included in the event (Mina, 2015).

The Irish soldiers Berro referred to were part of the United Nations Interim Force in Lebanon (UNIFIL), which was established by the United Nations in March 1978 in response to Israeli forces' invasion of Lebanon on the night of 14/15 March 1978. The first UNIFIL troops arrived in the area on 23 March 1978 and were organised for three broadly defined purposes: to confirm the withdrawal of Israeli forces, to restore international peace and security and to assist the Lebanese government in ensuring the return of its effective authority in the area (UNIFIL, 2019a).

Ireland, now one of the leading rugby union nations in the world, belongs to the countries contributing troops to UNIFIL. In February 2019, there were 462 Irish soldiers in Lebanon. UNIFIL's force consisted at this point of a total of 10,303 peacekeepers from 42 countries (UNIFIL, 2019b). Until 2018, Fijian soldiers were also a part of UNIFIL, with the last batch that left the country in December 2018 consisting of 134 soldiers (UNIFIL, 2019c).

> In June 1996 we played the first game via Fijian UNIFIL Battalion in Tyre, South Lebanon; the match was called Qana Memorial Cup, in memory of the tragic events at the Fijian Battalion HQ in Qana on the 18th of April, 1996.
>
> remembered Jammal

Although the first official rugby union match in Lebanon was played in 1995, some players had already been exposed to the sport through the scout movement. As we learned in conversation with Nadim Abboud, the Scouts of Jamhour started playing flag rugby in 1988. Abboud served at this time as a troop chief. The games were played in the 10 versus 10 and 20 versus 20 formats, and tournaments with hundreds of participants were organised. Among Catholic scouts, 'Scout Rugby' is still common today and has become part of an annual tournament held by the Saint Joseph School in Cornet Chahwan. Some rugby scout players played a major role in establishing the Jamhour rugby club. The scouts are still important today for Lebanese rugby union. When asked where they were first exposed to rugby, the majority of the Under 18 national men's team players said it was through being scouts. While this means that a majority of players are Christians, there are still a considerable number of Muslim players in rugby union, contributing to a cross-religious understanding in the divided country.

Developing women's rugby union in Lebanon

The story of the establishment of women's rugby union in Lebanon is different than that of men's game, although there is one similarity: foreign influence. 'Most girls started playing two weeks prior to the match and had never played a union game before', remembered Sarah Aouad. She was one of the players who participated in the two matches against the Egyptian team in 2012 (both matches were lost). While for most of the women rugby was new, some had been exposed to it in the scout movement.

What differentiates the first generation of female players from the first cohort of male players is that for most of these women, the sport was totally new, while many men had been exposed to it while living in England, France or other rugby union strongholds. However, there is still some external influence in Lebanese women's rugby union: the coach of the female national team, Amady Diallo, is Senegalese. He is the former captain of the Senegalese men's sevens team whose spouse is a UN diplomat in Lebanon. While Diallo gives instructions to his players in French, the coach of the men's team, Steve Wrigglesworth, a former British navy soldier who lives in Cyprus, communicates to his players in English, reflecting the cosmopolitan composition of Lebanon, a country in which it is common to be tri-lingual (in Arabic, French and English).

When this research was conducted, there were about 180 registered rugby union players in Lebanon, with approximately 30% of them women. While female rugby union development in Lebanon is focusing on rugby sevens, there are both 15-a-side and sevens national teams at the men's level and national youth teams in different formats as can be seen in Table 5.1.

There are five men's clubs in the country. Four of the five clubs participated in the 2018 domestic men's championship: Beirut Phoenicians, Froggies Beyrouth, Jounieh Dragons and Jamhour Black Lions,

Table 5.1 State of the art of rugby union in Lebanon (February 2019)

Population size	6,061,722
Country size	10,452 km^2
Population density	583 (per km^2)
Number of players	180 (men 130/women 50)
National teams	Men:
	XV's National team 'The Phoenix'
	XV's B team 'Phoenix Select'
	7's
	U 18 (XV)
	U 16 (X)
	U 14 (7's)
	Women:
	7's National
	7's Development
Number of clubs	5 men
	2 women
Number of schools offering rugby union	5 (private schools)
	3 have a girl's programme (one of them is a mixed team)
Number of universities offering rugby union	1 private university (programme is only for women)

Sources: World Population Review, 2019; author's own elaboration.

with the latter winning the 2018 championship. The two women's teams were established in 2017 (Blue Stars) and 2018 (Beirut Aconites). The founders of one of the two women's clubs, the Blue Stars, were scouts. The Blue Stars and Beirut Aconites planned a series of matches against each other to determine the first Lebanese women's champion in 2019. In November 2018, a Palestinian refugee women's team was established and played a friendly match against the Beirut Aconites. All of the men's and women's teams play on pitches that are also used for football.

Although Lebanon's society is more liberal than that of other Arab countries, women's rugby in Lebanon also faces cultural barriers. As national team player Zina Ibrahim said in Enzo Baudino's film *One Nation*, a documentary about Lebanese rugby union: 'It is so hard to get women for a contact sport in Lebanon, it is almost impossible. For many parents it is out of the question. I was called a lesbian' (Baudino, 2018). Other female players interviewed in the film said many people in Lebanon associate rugby with violence and masculinity. Apart from the cultural barriers for women, female players also made positive statements about the role of rugby in Lebanese society, for example, by stating that it is 'the only sport where we don't talk about religion, politics, region' (Baudino, 2018). This is a relevant aspect, since the argument is made in academic literature (e.g. Nassif and Amara, 2015; Reiche, 2011) that clubs in the two major sports in Lebanon, football and basketball, are clearly linked to certain political parties and religions. However, Blanc (2005) and Nassif (2013) have argued that both codes of rugby are more independent. One of the male players, 'Big Mo', interviewed for this research, confirmed: 'There is only one "religion": rugby. We don't care about religions and politics'.

A growing sport

A milestone for rugby union in Lebanon was when one of the most watched private television channels in the country, the Lebanese Broadcasting Corporation International (LBCI), broadcast the final of the West Asian men's rugby union Division 3 championship in 2018, which was hosted by Lebanon in the coastal city of Jounieh. Lebanon won the final against Iran, with Qatar and Jordan also competing in the tournament.

Another promising indicator for the growth of rugby union in Lebanon is the fact that five high schools have incorporated rugby union into their Physical Education (PE) curriculum. All of the schools are private, international schools: two French (Collège Notre-Dame in Jamhour and Collège Saint Joseph in Antoura) and three American (American Community School Beirut, Brummana High School and International College Beirut). The International College Beirut is Lebanon's largest high school with around 3,500 students. Most of the school coaches are international faculty from countries such as Argentina, France, Senegal, United Kingdom and United States.

There are two main challenges for Lebanese rugby union. The first is to integrate rugby union into public-school PE curricula, although two out of three pupils in Lebanon go to a private high school. The second is gaining presence in universities. Apart from rugby sevens, which is currently played by female students at the AUB, no other university has a rugby union programme. However, this does not mean that university students are not interested in rugby; they just choose another code: rugby league.

Benefitting from rugby league

Rugby at the AUB, home of the only university rugby union women's team, started as rugby league. Due to the lack of competition, however (the only other women's rugby league team at Lebanese American

University (LAU) dissolved prior to the 2018/2019 season), the AUB women's team switched to rugby union sevens. On the other hand, the male students at AUB play rugby league in two teams and are participating in the 2018/2019 season in the Collegiate Rugby League (CRL) Division 1 as one out of five universities (with Beirut Arab University, LAU, Notre Dame University Louaize and University of Balamand) and in Division 2 as one out of three teams (with Lebanese International University Tripoli and Lebanese International University Beirut; LRLF, 2019a, 2019b).

The example of the AUB women's team shows that rugby union in Lebanon has benefitted from rugby league. There are several examples of players who were first exposed to rugby league before deciding to play union. Switching codes in Lebanon is widespread among players, with some players active in both codes. Rugby league is more popular in Lebanon than rugby union: As of February 2019, there were approximately 450 rugby league players, said us Remond Safi from the LRLF.

The Lebanese rugby league national men's team has participated in the World Cups of 2000 and 2017, a success that is, at this point, unthinkable for Lebanese rugby union. However, when Lebanon participated for the first time in the Rugby League World Cup (RLWC) in 2000, the sport was non-existent in the country, and the team was entirely comprised of Australians of Lebanese descent who had formed a team in the late 1990s in Sydney to participate in international matches (Reiche, 2018). In 2017, the team consisted again of Australians with Lebanese heritage, although this time there was one Lebanon-based player in the squad. However, it should be mentioned that his inclusion was rather a symbolic act; he sat on the bench for all matches without playing a single minute (Reiche, 2018).

What has changed between Lebanon's participation in the 2000 and 2017 RLWCs is that a remarkable domestic development took place which set the ground for the growth of both codes of rugby in Lebanon. Apart from the university teams referred to earlier in this chapter, there is a Schools Rugby League (SRL) Championship, divided into two championships based on regions, with the North Division and Mount Lebanon Division competing in separate championships. In the 2018/2019 season, there were nine schools participating, five in the North division and four in the Mount Lebanon division.

How can the success of rugby league in Lebanon be explained? In the main global rugby league strongholds, the two Australian states of New South Wales and Queensland as well as northern England, the sport developed in working-class environments (Collins, 2013).

One example is a club from the Sydney suburb Belmore, where the Canterbury-Bankstown Bulldogs are well known for their popularity among the Lebanese-Australian community (Tabar, Noble, and Poynting, 2010). However, in Lebanon, rugby league became popular at private universities rather than in working-class environments such as Belmore.

According to Danny Kazandjian, who came to Lebanon in 2002 to develop rugby league, this was a pragmatic decision considering the lack of rugby league infrastructure in the country: 'We had no resources while the universities had the facilities and budget to run a championship' (in Reiche, 2018, p. 460). 'Danny walked into my office in 2002 and convinced me to set up a rugby league program at LAU', remembers the Director of Athletics at LAU of Beirut (in Reiche, 2018, p. 460). The successful launch of rugby league programmes at private Lebanese universities can be considered as 'path dependency' (Bengtsson, 2012, p. 161). It might be difficult for the Lebanese rugby union community to change the trajectory of rugby league continuing to be the dominant code at Lebanese universities.

Domestic and external recognition

The LRUF was recognised by the Lebanese government in 2009 – 14 years after the first Lebanese team match against the British navy team and 4 years after a federation establishment committee was formed. According to the requirements of the Lebanese Ministry of Youth and Sports, four clubs were needed in order to obtain federation status. The first club that obtained an official club licence by the Ministry was the Beirut Phoenicians in 2005. In 2009, four rugby union clubs were finally operating in Lebanon, and the federation received the long-awaited government recognition. The LRFU mission statement wants 'to raise awareness of Rugby Union in Lebanon by advancing the game in Schools and Universities with a goal of leading Lebanon towards the 2016 Olympic Games' (LRUF, 2011).

In 2009, after gaining recognition from the government, LRUF also became an associate member of the Asian Rugby Union Federation. The Lebanese national men's sevens team participated in the 2014 Asian Games in South Korea, winning one out of five matches and ending the tournament ranked 10 out of the 12 participating countries. Although Lebanon did not qualify for the 2016 Olympic Games in Rio or the 2018 Asian Games in Indonesia, it made progress in gaining domestic and international recognition.

In July 2010, members of the Federation and players of the national team met Lebanon's President Michel Suleiman, who

> was particularly impressed with the fact that the team transcends all religious or political bias; it comprises Christians, Sunnis, Shiites, Druze, and even one Palestinian. In recognition of this, we have since added 'One Nation' immediately below our national emblem on our player shirts.
>
> (LRUF, 2011)

In 2011, LRUF received for the first time a government grant of 16,500 USD: 'Although the amount given only scratches the surface of our seasonal budget, this kind action was very encouraging', stated an internal LRFU document. The document also noted:

> the main source of funding has been through one individual, our Chairman (Abdallah Ali Jammal, CEO of Jammal Trust Bank and other business corporations). It is his vision and financial support that has helped establish our standing in world Rugby Union today.
>
> (LRUF, 2011)

As opposed to rugby league, rugby union is recognised by the International Olympic Committee (IOC). LRUF, unlike the LRLF, has been a member of the Lebanese National Olympic Committee (LOC) since rugby union with its shortened version of rugby sevens was readmitted to the Olympic programme for the 2016 Games. In May 2010, LRUF became one of 28 federations allowed to vote in the general assembly of the LOC. Mazen Ramadan from the LOC told us that the inclusion has tremendous benefits for the federation and that 'Being an Olympic sport, they have a big advantage of benefiting from Olympic solidarity programs. And because of limited resources of the LOC, non-Olympic sports are not benefiting from our support'.

In 2017, LRUF successfully applied through the LOC for a $30,000 grant from Olympic Solidarity for the Development of National Sports Structures. Olympic Solidarity is a programme of the IOC 'created more than 50 years ago in order to assist newly independent countries, particularly in Asia and Africa, to develop their own structures to favour the expansion of sport at national level' (Olympic Solidarity, 2019). The Olympic Solidarity grant was spent for coaching courses (that included, apart from Lebanese and Syrian participants), a First Aid in Rugby course for physiotherapists and doctors, pitch fees for women's and youth tournaments as well as a 'get into rugby' event for Palestinian refugee children (Wrigglesworth, 2018).

In November 2018, LRUF was awarded associate member status by World Rugby, becoming 1 out of 123 federations in the global rugby union organisation (Asia Rugby, 2018). To become an associate member of World Rugby, countries are required to have national men's fifteens and sevens sides teams and a women's national sevens team. A women's 15-a-side team is not mandatory for recognition as an associate or full member (World Rugby, 2017). One obstacle in the process of becoming an associate member of World Rugby had been the slow development of women's rugby in Lebanon. The before-mentioned match against an Egyptian squad in 2012 did not lead to the sustainable development of women's rugby in the country. But in April 2018, during the West Asian Rugby Division 3 men's championship, a women's tournament was organised by LRUF, with Qatar (who won the tournament), Syria (third place) and two Lebanese teams (second and fourth rank) playing. This paved the way for LRUF to finally become an associate member of World Rugby in November 2018. According to Douha Knio, at the April 2018 tournament 'almost all of us were locals' and only one of the 24 players was living abroad.

Associate members are entitled

> to participate in competitions on a qualified basis, to be decided by the Regional Association in consultation with the World Rugby (not including RWC tournaments); attendance at the biennial General Assembly in a non-voting capacity; receipt of World Rugby Publications; access to World Rugby Administrative advice/support.

While no direct World Rugby Funding will be provided to Associate Members, World Rugby funding to support agreed projects to be considered on a case by case basis is possible (World Rugby, 2017).

To obtain full membership status, 'after 2 Years (24 months) of Associate Membership of the World Rugby a Union may apply to become a Full Member of the World Rugby' (World Rugby, 2017). The main advantage of full membership status for LRUF would be that the federation could apply for World Rugby development grants and would become a voting member in the General Assembly. However, there is one main difference between qualifying for full rather than associate member status. While associate membership only requires a federation to 'have an annual domestic adult male fifteen a-side competition with a minimum of 4 teams', full member status requires a federation to have the same competition with a minimum of ten teams (World Rugby, 2017). In the 2018 Lebanese rugby union championship, four teams participated.

Diaspora recruitment

As in other sports, citizenship qualifies players in both codes of rugby to represent a country. What is unique about rugby league and rugby union is that citizenship is not the only criterion that makes participation within a national team possible. There are two other options: proof of ancestry, defined as citizenship of parents or grandparents, and proof of residency. The latter is defined by World Rugby as a 'sporting naturalisation procedure, based on a geographical/presence test' (World Rugby, 2016, p. 163). The residency requirement used to be set at three years in both codes before rugby league decided in 2016 to increase this period to five years (RLIF, 2016). Rugby union finally did the same when it announced in 2017 a residency requirement of 60 months starting 31 December 2020. One of us, Axel Maugendre, is benefitting from the residency criterion. As a former rugby union player in the French fourth division, he came to Lebanon in September 2015 as a student. Three years later, he was for the first time nominated for the Lebanese national rugby union team. In the past, the residency rule also allowed some Palestinians residing in Lebanon to represent the national 15-a-side team, The Phoenix.

The Lebanese rugby union national men's team is less reliant on diaspora players than the national rugby league team. As Table 5.2 shows, 16 out of 26 players in the Lebanese squad for the West Asian Division 3 championship in April 2018 were players of the Lebanese clubs Beirut Phoenicians, Jamhour Black Lions and Jounieh Spartans. All of those players are amateurs. As opposed to the national rugby league men's team, which entirely depends on Lebanese-Australians, only 3 out of 26 players in the national rugby union team were from Australian clubs. The other seven foreigners played for clubs in England (4), France (2) and the United States (1), mostly on a semi-professional level. Eighteen of the 26 players were Lebanese citizens, while 8 players qualified through their ancestry (one of the players qualified through both residency and ancestry). The Head Coach of the national team noted that 'We are looking to build our future national squad on up-and-coming Lebanese based players and overseas players who we can identify by engaging with overseas Lebanese communities'.

Table 5.2 Lebanon's squad at the 2018 men's West Asian Division 3 championship

	Name	Club (country)	Eligible through
1	Tariq Al Khaldi	Barnes RFC (England)	Ancestry
2	Cyril Irani	Jamhour Black Lions (Lebanon)	Citizenship
3	Louis Fyad	Stade Langonnais Rugby (France)	Ancestry
4	Rohan Zebib	Eastwood RFC (Australia)	Ancestry
5	Mohammad Turk	Ruby Club Des Angles (France)	Citizenship
6	Robbie Farjalla	Beirut Phoenicians (Lebanon)	Citizenship
7	Raymon Finan	Beirut Phoenicians (Lebanon)	Citizenship
8	Mounir Finan	Beirut Phoenicians (Lebanon)	Citizenship
9	Jean Michel Rizk	Jamhour Black Lions (Lebanon)	Citizenship
10	Sol Mokdad	Beirut Phoenicians (Lebanon)	Citizenship
11	Frank Fournier	San Diego Legion (USA)	Ancestry
12	Joseph Touma	London Irish Wild Geese RFC (England)	Citizenship
13	Camil Abou Farhat	Jamhour Black Lions (Lebanon)	Citizenship
14	Omar El Hout	Beirut Phoenicians (Lebanon)	Citizenship
15	Karim Jammal	Beirut Phoenicians (Lebanon)	Citizenship
16	Lawrence Abood	Southport RFC (England)	Ancestry
17	Ben Abood	West Harbour RFC (Australia)	Ancestry
18	Laurent Zalloum	Jamhour Black Lions (Lebanon)	Citizenship
19	Martin Wahbe	Hunters Hill RC (Australia)	Ancestry
20	Omar Hamaoui	Jamhour Black Lions (Lebanon)	Citizenship
21	Steve Pere	Jounieh Spartans (Lebanon)	Ancestry and residency
22	Hazem El Tawil	Beirut Phoenicians (Lebanon)	Citizenship
23	George Rahal	Jamhour Black Lions (Lebanon)	Citizenship
24	Robin Hachache	Jamhour Black Lions (Lebanon)	Citizenship
25	Ibrahim Ballout	Beirut Phoenicians (Lebanon)	Citizenship
26	Raymond Asfour	Old Cofeians RFC (England)	Citizenship

Conclusion

The development of rugby union in Lebanon is promising. Played for the first time in 1995, it was successfully established as a new sport in the country, recognised domestically by the Lebanese Ministry of Youth and Sports and the National Olympic Committee and internationally as an associate member of World Rugby. Compared to rugby league, the more popular and more successful rugby code in Lebanon, union has in the long term some advantages, such as the ability to access funds from Olympic Solidarity and the opportunity to qualify for both the Asian Games and the Olympic Games. The national men's union team is less reliant on diaspora players than the national men's league team, while women's rugby in both codes is mainly shaped by locally grown players. Rugby union in Lebanon missed the opportunity to become a college sport unlike rugby league, which is played at several private universities. Apart from this, both league and union face similar challenges, particularly a lack of infrastructure and a reliance on football fields, a lack of sufficient governmental support and private sponsors and the challenge of developing both codes in public schools.

Given the small pool of rugby players in Lebanon (by February 2019 around 630 in both codes), we believe that there should be more cooperation between the Lebanese rugby union and rugby league federations. This could happen through, for example, the coordination of league and union seasons to allow players to participate in both championships and through recruitment of rugby league players for sevens to grant the opportunity to qualify for events such as the Asian Games and the Olympic Games. Unfortunately, there is little communication between the two federations and even some degree of hostility, although many players are less dogmatic and have been active in both codes.

If rugby union wants to grow globally and expand to the periphery, the sport needs to develop beyond its traditional centres. Meeting World Rugby's full membership requirement of having a local men's competition with at least ten teams (which would allow access to development funds) is not realistically possible for a tiny, developing country like Lebanon with limited sporting infrastructure. If World Rugby does not change this requirement, countries like Lebanon will remain second-class citizens in the global rugby union community.

References

AEFE (2019). Rechercher un établissement. Available at www.aefe.fr/reseau-scolaire-mondial/rechercher-un-etablissement

Asia Rugby (2018). Lebanon welcomed as associate members of World Rugby. Available at www.asiarugby.com/2018/11/15/associate-members-of-world-rugby/

Baudino, E. (2018). *One Nation*. Available at www.youtube.com/watch?v=-FwnpdHjl_Q&feature=youtu.be

Bengtsson, B. (2012). Path dependency. In S. J. Smith (Ed.) *International encyclopedia of housing and home*. Amsterdam: Elsevier (pp. 161–166).

Blanc, P. (2005). Le sport au Liban: Un révélateur de la société. In K. Gjeloshaj and C. Chiclet (Eds.) *Sport et politique en Méditérrannée*. Paris: L'harmattan (pp. 159–162).

Collins, T. (2013). *Rugby's great split: Class, culture and the origins of rugby league football*. Abingdon: Routledge.

LRUF (2011). In partnership with Lebanese rugby union. Unpublished manuscript, Beirut: Lebanese Rugby Union Federation.

LRLF (2019a). Collegiate rugby league division 1. Available at http://lebanonrl.com/Championships/Collegiate-Rugby-League/Division1
LRLF (2019b). Collegiate rugby league division 2. Available at http://lebanonrl.com/Championships/Collegiate-Rugby-League/Division2
Mina, Z. (2015). *Les Jeux de la Francophonie de Beyrouth (2009), analyseurs du système sportif libanais.* Lyon: Université Claude Bernard Lyon I.
Nassif, N. (2013). *Analyse de la politique du sport au Liban (1991/2012).* Grenoble: Université de Grenoble.
Nassif, N., and Amara, M. (2015). Sport, policy and politics in Lebanon. *International Journal of Sport Policy and Politics*, 7(3), 443–455.
Olympic Solidarity (2019). Olympic solidarity. Available at www.olympic.org/olympic-solidarity
Reiche, D. (2011). War minus the shooting? The politics of sport in Lebanon as a unique case in comparative politics. *Third World Quarterly*, 32(2), 261–277.
Reiche, D. (2018). The role of the Lebanese-Australian diaspora in the establishment of rugby league in Lebanon. *The International Journal of the History of Sport*, 35(5), 448–467.
RLIF (2016). Eligibility for international Rugby league. Available at http://www.rlif.com/ignite_docs/20160920%20RLIF%20Eligibility%20Rules%20-%20Final.pdf
Tabar, P., Noble, G., and Poynting, S. (2010). *On being Lebanese in Australia: Identity, racism and the ethnic field.* Beirut: Lebanese American University Press.
UNIFIL (2019a). UNIFIL Background. Available at https://unifil.unmissions.org/unifil-background
UNIFIL (2019b). Troop contributing countries. Available at https://unifil.unmissions.org/unifil-troop-contributing-countries
UNIFIL (2019c). Fijian troops conclude UNIFIL mission. Available at https://unifil.unmissions.org/fijian-troops-conclude-unifil-mission
World Rugby (2016). Regulation 8. Available at www.worldrugby.org/wr-resources/WorldRugbyDIR/Handbook/English/pubData/source/files/Regulation8.pdf
World Rugby (2017). World Rugby membership pathway. Available at https://pulse-static-files.s3.amazonaws.com/worldrugby/document/2017/09/08/9bb65338-65d2-463f-b0f4-26ec5bea53d3/150505-CL-World-Rugby-Membership-Pathway-and-Criteria-English.pdf
Wrigglesworth, S. (2018). Olympic solidarity funding report: Lebanese Rugby Union federation. Unpublished manuscript. Beirut: Lebanese Rugby Union.

6 'Moufflons' living precariously
The brief history of rugby union in Cyprus

Mike Rayner

Introduction

This chapter considers the contemporary evolution of the game of rugby union in Cyprus, specifically focussing on the political influences on sport within the country, the continual adaptations made to the sport of rugby union and the increased influence of television companies, sponsors and the media more generally that have impacted upon the game in Cyprus. This chapter is constructed around themes that have emerged through interviews with current and former elite rugby union players who have represented Cyprus, as well as with British Servicemen and coaches/managers currently involved in the game within the country. Consequently, the anonymity of the participants was ensured through the use of pseudonyms.

Colonialism, education and sporting developments within Cyprus

> Heaven bless the isle of Cyprus and our noble general Othello!
> (Shakespeare, 2006, 2.2.10–11)

Cyprus is an island in the eastern Mediterranean and is a place of strategic and historic importance. According to Kartakoullis, Kriemadis and Pouloukas (2009, p. 228):

> Cyprus has been controlled by most of the major powers that had interest in, or sought control of, the Middle East. The list of its successive rulers included the Egyptians, Greeks, Phoenicians, Assyrians, Persians, Ptolemies, Romans, Byzantines, Franks, Venetians, Ottoman Turks and British.

Most of its population is of Greek descent, with other large ethnic groups including Turkish and Armenian, as well as large communities of European and non-European citizens (Maniou, 2017).

The British rule of Cyprus began in 1878 when Cyprus was placed under the United Kingdom's (UK) administration as part of the Cyprus Convention and then it became a formally annexed military occupation in 1914. In 1959, following a sustained period of violence within the country, representatives from the UK, Greece, Turkey and several local Cypriot community leaders met to discuss the London and Zurich Agreements in order to form the constitution of Cyprus. Consequently, Cyprus became an independent state and part of the United Nations in August 1960.

The rich and diverse demographic history of the island's population formed the basis of the constitution and ultimately the island's claim for independence. The constitution divided the population into distinct communities based on their ethnic origin and stipulated that the President had to be a Greek-Cypriot elected by Greek-Cypriots and the Vice-President a Turkish-Cypriot elected by Turkish-Cypriots. It was believed that the constitution formally recognised the two different ethnic groups and their languages but also guaranteed political rights and state offices for both Greek- and Turkish-Cypriot communities (Shaw, 2014). However, the segregation of the population caused the social situation on the island to deteriorate further and increased inter-communal violence throughout much of the 1960s. On 15 July 1974, an Athens-sponsored coup by Greek-Cypriot paramilitaries ousted the president, Archbishop Makarios (Kıralp, 2017). Five days later, Turkey retaliated by invading and during a short but bloody conflict occupied the northern third of the island until a truce was brokered on 30 July 1974. Consequently, a clear boundary was formed dividing the country between the Greek-Cypriots in the South and the Turkish-Cypriots in the North.

Despite this constant societal upheaval, sport became an unbroken value among all communities in Cyprus. While Cyprus obtained its independence in 1960, it had previously been under British rule for 82 years, the development of sport followed the same path in Cyprus as it did in other countries within the British Empire. The movement of British servicemen, their families, traders, administrators, engineers and all the accompanying trades and occupations associated with colonisation enabled their cultural cargo, language, tastes and sporting interests and pursuits to be disseminated throughout foreign lands (Rayner, 2017). As a result, the various versions of British sports such as cricket, horseracing and the different variations of football soon spread to areas of British influence overseas including Cyprus (Black and Nauright, 1998).

The first games of football in Cyprus were recorded in 1900 with the local newspaper *The Voice of Cyprus*, noting that

> thirty distinguished young men, away from political conflicts, are gathering twice a week in a specific place and in an English manner, they are exercising in football – a nice and deeply athletic activity, which is largely growing against all other sports.
>
> (in Maniou, 2017, p. 128)

While the volume of participants documented in the article replicates the numbers utilised in the modern game of rugby union, this report specifically illustrates an emphasis on 'Englishness' which also suggests that the participants were from the upper class and potentially consisted of the British colonists on the island participating in the game (Appadurai, 1995).

In 1911, the first Greek-Cypriot association football team, named Anorthosis of Famagusta, was formed. By 1934, both Greek and Turkish communities were involved in setting up the Cyprus Football Association (CFA) and forming clubs around the country to participate in an all-island league. Despite interruption due to Second World War, the all-island league was popular among all communities, and in 1948, the CFA became an associate member of the Union of European Football Associations (UEFA). However, in 1955, the deterioration of the social situation within the country led to the Turkish-Cypriot clubs splitting away from the CFA and forming their own independent governing body: Kıbrıs Türk Futbol Federasyonu (KTFF). Despite the spilt between the two communities, both the CFA and the KTFF regularly organised international matches with the KTFF recorded as participating in matches against Saudi Arabia, Malaysia and Libya. However, it was only the CFA that was recognised by UEFA, and in 1962, the CFA was awarded full membership to the governing body. This left the KTFF in international isolation as the federation was not recognised by UEFA which meant that they could not compete in international competitions.

The growth of the rugby union game on the island underwent a similar yet distinctly different trajectory to that of association football. Although association football was initially popularised along relatively informal lines among the native population, rugby union's popularity was heavily reliant upon the education system introduced into the country during British colonisation. The period of British rule in Cyprus from 1878 until 1960 coincided with a transformation in the scale and nature of Britain's sporting culture (Tranter, 1998). Scholars (e.g. Dunning and Sheard, 1979; Golby, 1988; Hobsbawn, 1990) have suggested that the heritage of the games of football and rugby emerged out of conflict and rivalry between English public schools in the early to mid-nineteenth century. This conflict led to competition between the schools, and while the rivalry was not necessarily on the playing field, it became a tool for the measurement and societal status of the public schools within wider society (Hobsbawm, 1983).

According to Shaw (2014), as well as education being provided within both the Greek-Cypriot and Turkish-Cypriot communities, the British developed schools modelled on the public-school system in England that offered a British curriculum with a view to having their students accepted into universities in the UK. Shaw (2014) further describes a British colonial official introducing a range of sports into a British designed public-school curriculum on the island. While Shaw (2014) illustrates that athletic competitions took place annually across the island in sports such as association football, hockey and cricket, he also notes that the school had historically strong ties with the universities of Cambridge and Oxford. It was at these two institutions in which the modification of the competing football rules first took place during the nineteenth century. At Cambridge, the dominance of ex-public schoolboys from the most established and elite schools, including Eton and Harrow, ensured that the 'kicking' rules referred to as football became adopted as the rules in university matches (Rayner, 2017). Consequently, while the work of Shaw refers to the British educational system enhancing the participation and profile of association football, it also serves to illustrate the influence of the 'old boys' network and the development of a range of schools modelled on the British public-school system whereby staff influenced curriculums, sporting endeavours and the overall development of the sporting landscape within Cyprus.

The increasing aspiration of the Cypriot communities to send their children to schools modelled on the British public-school system and onto UK universities amplified during the periods of hostility in 1950s and again after the island gained independence in 1960. The emergence of sport scholarships into the British public-school system provided not only the obvious educational opportunities, but it also created a body of prototype sport migrants (Horton, 2012). These opportunities facilitated an increase in the number of students educated within British-led schools, often returning to their communities to teach sport to their compatriots. For example, Tom Wills, who was born in

Australia, was educated at Rugby school and Cambridge University before returning to Australia whereby he established the first football club in Melbourne (Collins, 2009). Wills used his British educational experiences to establish the sport in Melbourne adapting several of the original Rugby school rules, although the main regulations were followed. These variations are of major cultural significance for Australian sport as they have been symbolised within the process of developing an independent national sport in Australia (Australian Rules football). However, while the example of Tom Wills dates to a period before British rule in Cyprus, it serves to note the importance of colonisation and the impact of the British educational system on the development of sport.

As previously mentioned, it was both the British military and its political influence that had an impact on the game of rugby union within Cyprus. The game itself was first introduced to the country by British servicemen serving on the two 'Sovereign Base Areas', Akrotiri and Dhekelia, that were kept by the British as part of the agreement for granting Cyprus independence in 1960. While initially rugby union remained isolated to the military bases and played predominately among British personnel, there was some noticeable engagement from the local population during the late 1950s. In a similar guise to the establishment of rugby union in North America during 1895, whereby officers at a British Army garrison based in Montréal socialised with students from the local McGill University (Collins, 2009); a relationship between British servicemen and the local community began to form during the late 1950s and 1960s which serves as the foundation of the rugby union game on the island of Cyprus:

> You see, unlike other countries that were under British rule, Cyprus wasn't really designed that way. There was such a diverse population which kind of defined what Cyprus was about, not Britain or its empire really. So when we started playing rugby on the base or even on the beach at Episkopi the locals were just intrigued but not really interested. It took a while but probably towards the end of my second tour there (British Military deployment), 1968–69, they started getting involved with the game. Back on my first tour in 1958 some of the locals got involved but they were mainly second generation 'British' Cypriots playing with us but there was a definite shift in interest in the 60s – probably enjoyed watching us British beat each other up and then having a go themselves!
>
> (Stephen)

> Obviously it (rugby union) wasn't as popular as football – they had a national team for that – but certainly during the 60s some of the boys who had been to British schools on the island or back home started to get involved and we would explain the rules and just play as well as we could. It wasn't worth going into detail about all the rules, which actually kept changing at the time, as football was their preferred choice but there was a noticeable transference from intrigue to interest in rugby union throughout the time I was there.
>
> (Trevor)

However, the internal unrest throughout the 1960s, which resulted in the Turkish invasion in 1974, caused many of the population, who were proficient English speakers through the previously discussed British influenced educational system, to emigrate to Anglophone countries such as the UK, South Africa, New Zealand and Australia. Consequently, throughout the 1970s and 1980s, rugby union became a game isolated in participation to the British servicemen on the 'Sovereign Base Areas' which ultimately restricted the development of the game among the local population.

> The invasion in 74 didn't help the game on the island. The numbers of English-speaking boys around the place dropped and people became measured on they nationally. That meant the Cypriot boys that stayed around played football as that became the adopted game within the country for some reason. So we just played amongst ourselves on the base, inter-services type stuff.
>
> (Paul)

Nonetheless, the island's population increased during the 1990s with a number of second-generation Cypriot nationals returning to the island due to the diffusion in political hostility between the Greek and Turkish-Cypriot communities. It is important to note this flow of returning expatriates to Cyprus during the 1990s as their experiences in Anglophone countries coincided with the game of rugby union being exposed to a range of developments within the media industry, professionalism and the transference to a business ethos within sport during the latter decades of the twentieth century that exposed rugby union to the realities of commercialism and the influences of a more diverse participating and spectating public. These returning expatriates had first-hand exposure of rugby union becoming a sport that embraced the demands of the commercial and entertainment sectors in order to survive and develop in the modern sporting environment.

Additionally, they had experienced the game in a range of global environments as both an amateur and professional sport and these experiences had an influence upon the next stage of development for the rugby union game in Cyprus.

Developing the Moufflons

During the final two decades of the twentieth century, rugby union's global profile and economic capital increased. The introduction of the Rugby World Cup (RWC) in 1987 and the close association with television coverage and sponsors occurred at a time when media expansion, through telecommunication developments, created a sellers' market for the sport (Ford and Ford, 1993). By the time of the second RWC in 1991, the demands of television and the commercial exigencies of media sport became even more dominant (Rayner, 2017). Consequently, the 1995 RWC was the last competition in which the 'elite' players performed as amateurs and the game became a professional sport on 27 August 1995.

The growth of rugby union's global profile through television and professionalisation had a direct impact upon the game within Cyprus. The volume of returning second-generation Cypriot nationals enabled the game to move from being a sport that had become isolated within the 'Sovereign Base Areas' to one that had a growing profile within the local community. In 2003, the first native civilian rugby union team was formed, the Paphos Tigers, who competed in friendly fixtures against the British military sides before officially joining the Joint Service Rugby Football Union league system. A further native team, the Limassol Crusaders, was also formed towards the end of 2003 as a result of the success and profile of England's RWC victory that year. The Limassol Crusaders joined the Paphos Tigers in the Joint Service Rugby Football Union league system for the 2004/2005 season and both teams currently compete in the annual competition.

> It was certainly an interesting time to be involved in rugby on the island. I had been in and out of the country for both school and work, so pretty much played the game wherever I could but never really had much to do with the game in Cyprus. So, when the two local teams were formed, we suddenly had an opportunity to play regularly rather than just in mini tournaments with the service teams or random one-off games. Don't get me wrong

we only played against military teams but at least we were representing ourselves rather than fitting into one of the teams on the bases.

(Mateo)

By 2006, the sustained popularity of rugby union on the island aided the development of the Cyprus Rugby Federation (CRF) to control the overall governance of rugby union within the country. During the same year, the CRF were tasked with developing a Cypriot national team and resultantly became an affiliated member of the Fédération Internationale de Rugby Amateur (FIRA) which was established in 1934 to administer rugby union in Europe. Consequently, on 24 March 2007, a Cyprus XV played against the Greece national team in Paphos, with the inaugural game seeing a 39-3 victory to the hosts in front of 2,500 spectators (McCowan, 2007). This seminal moment for international rugby union in Cyprus was the start of a successful period for the national team as through FIRA they were admitted into Group 3D of the 2006–2008 European Nations Cup. During the national team's first season in the tournament, Cyprus beat Azerbaijan, Monaco and Slovakia to win the 2006–2008 European Nations Cup Division 3D. However, despite suffering defeat in a play-off game to Israel for promotion to Division 3C for the 2008–2010 European Nations Cup, the Cypriot national team would continue their rapid growth to create a successful record over the next few years by playing 24 and winning 24: a world record sequence. The success created a profile of the national team both within domestic and international media and through a process of glocalisation the Cypriot national team were afforded a nickname by the native population of the island – the 'Moufflons' – which originates from a type of indigenous wild mountain sheep only found in Cyprus.

This successful period of rugby union within Cyprus was symbolic by the globalisation of sport that has occurred throughout the twentieth and twenty-first centuries with global flows of ideology, people, politics, economics and the media (Hajisoteriou and Angelides, 2018). The opportunity for international competition, the development of native rugby union clubs and the diffusion of hostilities between different the ethnic communities enabled the game of rugby union to develop a profile within the country. Furthermore, the rugby union game in Cyprus became symbolic of the global landscape of international rugby union whereby there has been a dramatic increase in the number of players playing international rugby union for countries other than their nation of birth. The opportunity of international competition, facilitated by the process of globalisation, has seen second- or even third-generation Cypriots choosing to play for Cyprus rather than play for their country of birth despite in some cases having never been to the island beforehand:

> My grandad was from Cyprus, which makes me a quarter Cypriot. I think I had been to island maybe a couple of times as a young kid but had no memories of the country. I got involved through a trial in London, played a 7s tournament in Georgia before actually arriving in Cyprus for my first home game which was realistically my first memory of the island itself. But how could I say no to playing international rugby? I had to go to a trail but as soon as I knew that there was a possibility, I didn't think twice.
>
> (Adrian)

Notwithstanding this period of success, rugby union in Cyprus was still played and administered by a small number of the population and in a relatively informal manner. While the major nations in world rugby were predominately professional, rugby union in Cyprus was established under amateur terms, and consequently, many of its players were drafted from the amateur game both within Cyprus and from around the world. Subsequently, the players were responsible for their own dietary plans, fitness regimes, playing kit, injury and recovery processes:

> I'm responsible for my own training, diet etc which is fine as I play for a local club here in England which ticks most of that off. However, I don't play at a particularly high level so when I turn out for Cyprus, sometimes the increase in standards can be a bit of a shock to the body. If I get injured that can mean time off work, which doesn't go down too well. Plus, when I do play for Cyprus, I need to use a big chunk of my annual leave and in the early days I had to arrange and pay for my own travel and accommodation. I'm happy to do that to play international rugby but it means my life is structured around work, rugby training and rugby games – very little time for anything else.
>
> (Alexandros)

Despite functioning as an amateur sport, the sequence of 24 wins for the Cypriot national team between 29 November 2008 and

1 November 2014 enabled the national team to progress from Group 3D to 2B of the European Nations Cup. However, this success did not provide the opportunity to qualify for the 2015 RWC as World Rugby rejected the CRF's application for membership to the game's global governing body. The national team were not eligible to participate in qualification rounds for the global tournament as they were not a full member of World Rugby, despite becoming a full member to FIRA (now known as Rugby Europe) and applying for associate membership to World Rugby in February 2012. Furthermore, World Rugby cited a lack of a four-team domestic 15-a-side league, which was a requirement stipulated in the Membership Pathway and Criteria. While Cyprus did have a have a seven-team 15-a-side league at the time, four of the sides were British Royal Air Force and Army teams located in the 'Sovereign Base Areas', technically playing on British soil and affiliated to the Rugby Football Union and not the CRF.

> That was kind of gutting, it genuinely felt like we had a chance to attempt to qualify for the World Cup. It's one of those governance things that were discussed well above me in the system, but I really thought they would let us try and go for it, especially after such a winning run.
>
> (Marios)

However, in 2014, World Rugby accepted the CRF's application to become an affiliate member. Membership to the game's global governing body provided the opportunity for Cyprus to undergo a structural review in order to progress to becoming a full member. Consequently, while a third native rugby club, The Nicosia Barbarians, was formed in 2013 and a fourth has recently formed, The Larnaca Spartans, the CRF need these two new clubs to cultivate a development pathway and compete regularly in order to address the domestic league requirements of World Rugby. While there are two established rugby union clubs in Northern Cyprus, The Cypriot Pumas and NEU Tigers, they are not affiliated to the CRF due to the island's continued divided border and consequently the two clubs are not recognised by World Rugby.

Nonetheless, while the CRF continue to review the domestic league structure, the national team underwent a complete transformation in the years following membership to World Rugby. Although the country still holds the world record for consecutive wins, the CRF were conscious that the team had swiftly progressed through Rugby Europe's league structure (currently competing in Rugby Europe's Conference

1 South competition) and needed an experienced coach in which to organise the national team. Consequently, the CRF appointed Andrew Binikos who had previous experience of Super Rugby and despite functioning in an amateur set up, he brought a professional attitude to the national team:

> It was a big thing for Cyprus rugby when Bini came in. He had a wealth of experience and introduced a variety of different training sessions such as strength and conditioning, video analysis, fitness assessments and the key things such as dietary plans. He's a good boy and you either buy into it or you don't get a game. Another thing he put in place was a bigger role for the sponsors. Previously we would get our own flights to and from games and be responsible for our kit etc, but Bini saw to it that flights/accommodation were sorted and didn't come out of a players pocket.
>
> (Luca)

The introduction of a 'professional' attitude towards rugby in Cyprus has re-established the significance of rugby sevens in the continued development of overall rugby union game on the island. While Cyprus first entered a team into the FIRA Sevens series in 2008 and have continually entered into the annual competition, the reintroduction of rugby sevens into the Olympics, the World Rugby Sevens Series and RWC Sevens provides opportunities for Tier 2 and 3 nations to get regular exposure to elite-level competition. The national sevens rugby team for Cyprus currently competes in Rugby Europe's Conference competition which is only two leagues away from the top division within Europe. However, the CRF must continue to develop both the 7- and 15-a-side games in order to ensure that the rugby union 'product' develops appeal within the country and enhances their application to full membership of World Rugby. While the two versions have remained different enough to meet the specific needs of their respective audiences, the development of sevens illustrates that rugby union has evolved and taken a changing public with it. The lure of the Olympics is a driving force for the development of global sport, and the CRF must use it as an opportunity to grow both versions of the game within Cyprus.

Additionally, in 2019, World Rugby announced plans for a Nations Championship to be introduced into the rugby union calendar in 2022. The proposal suggests a transformation of the international rugby union landscape and has asked the Six Nations Championship and The Rugby Championship to consider a promotion/relegation system within their competition models. This opportunity would enable the minor nations from around the world, including Cyprus, to aspire to compete at the top table of international rugby. These proposals are part of readdressing the qualification processes for the RWC and a collective approach towards the governance and sustainability of rugby union around the globe. However, as an affiliate member of World Rugby, Cyprus does not receive a significant level of finance from the governing body and despite the proposal for competition reform, Cyprus will still struggle to find its place in the competitive landscape of international rugby union under this proposal.

At present, the CRF are faced with a range of issues that need prioritising to ensure the continued development of the game on the island. There have been significant advancements regarding the introduction of rugby union into educational curriculums outside of British influenced schools on the island which has been aided by the profile and success of the 'Moufflons' in the media. This development is a significant step towards full membership of World Rugby as it is the first time in history where the game of rugby union on the island is not simply designed towards competition but also designed to be inclusive. This development has opened the game to both sexes which will enable the women's game to grow organically on the island.

Furthermore, while World Rugby's Nations Championship proposal provides an avenue for the national team to qualify for the RWC, the additional demands and expectations could be detrimental to the continued development of rugby union in Cyprus. While the increase in media attention and potential increase in income could benefit full members of World Rugby, it is the smaller nations, such as Cyprus, that could struggle for survival. The CRF have significantly advanced the game of rugby union in Cyprus in a relatively short time, however, to ensure that this development continues, they should prioritise growth rather than performance and seek to adhere to the full membership requirements of World Rugby so that the game develops a clear identity and establishes a future within the native communities on the island.

References

Appadurai, A. (1995). Playing with modernity: The decolonialization of Indian cricket. In C. Beckenridge (Ed.) *Consuming modernity. Public culture in a south Asian world*. Minneapolis, MN: University of Minneapolis Press (pp. 23–48).

Black, D., and Nauright, J. (1998). *Rugby and the South African nation*. Manchester: Manchester University Press.

Collins, T. (2009). *A social history of English Rugby Union*. Oxon: Routledge.
Dunning, E., and Sheard, K. (1979). *Barbarians, gentlemen and players: A sociological study of the development of rugby football*. Oxon: Routledge.
Ford, B., and Ford, J. (1993). *Television and sponsorship*. Oxford: Butterworth-Heinemann Ltd.
Golby, J. (1988). *Culture & society in Britain: 1850–1890*. Oxford: Oxford University Press.
Hajisoteriou, C., and Angelides, P. (2018). Developing and implementing policies of intercultural education in Cyprus in the context of globalisation. *The Cyprus Review*, 30(1), 353–367.
Hobsbawm, E. (1983). Mass-producing traditions: Europe, 1870–1914. In E. Hobsbawm and T. Ranger (Eds.) *The invention of tradition*. Cambridge: Cambridge University Press (pp. 263–307).
Hobsbawn, E. (1990). *Industry and empire*. London: Penguin.
Horton, P. (2012). Pacific islanders in global rugby: The changing currents of sports migration. *The International Journal of the History of Sport*, 29(17), 2388–2404.
Kartakoullis, N., Kriemadis, T., and Pouloukas, S. (2009). Cyprus: A football crazy nation? *Soccer & Society*, 10(2), 226–244.
Kıralp, Ş. (2017). Cyprus between enosis, partition and independence: Domestic politics, diplomacy and external interventions (1967–74). *Journal of Balkan and Near Eastern Studies*, 19(6), 591–609.
Maniou, T. (2017). Political conflicts in the Cypriot football fields: A qualitative approach through the press. *Soccer & Society*, 20(1), 123–138.
McCowan, A. (2007, March 27). Cyprus trounce Greece in first international match. *Cyprus Mail*, Available at https://web.archive.org/web/20070927203012/http://www.cyprus-mail.com/news/main.php?id=31510&archive=1
Rayner, M. (2017). *Rugby Union and professionalisation: Elite player perspectives*. Oxon: Routledge.
Shakespeare, W. (2006). *Othello*. Edited by Michael Neill. Oxford: Oxford University Press. 2.2.10–11.
Shaw, M. (2014). The Cyprus game: Crossing the boundaries in a divided island. *Globalisation, Societies and Education*, 12(2), 262–274.
Tranter, N. (1998). *Sport, economy and society in Britain 1750–1914*. Cambridge: Cambridge University Press.

7 Rugby and sport development in Brazil

From peripheral to centre stage

Gareth Hall and Arianne Reis

Introduction

This chapter builds on the 'Sport Works' narrative adopted in Sport-for-Development (SfD) programmes. In doing so, one SfD case in Brazil, that is utilising the sport of rugby to foster positive social transformation in its participants, communities and society, is examined to demonstrate the ways in which rugby is making a difference. To help situate the unique context in which rugby developed in Brazil a short socio-historical context demonstrates the sport's remarkable ability to 'hold' on with never more than 1,000 players at any given time in its history (up until 1997), increasing to approximately 3,000 players by 2007. Although a thorough overview for the historical development of rugby in Brazil, and in particular SfD, is beyond the scope of this chapter (see Schulenkorf, Sherry and Rowe, 2016, for a more extensive review of SfD), some socio-historical context is required to locate rugby and SfD's importance as an extension of broader changes in social conventions and attitudes towards sport.

Try Rugby is a large-scale inter-organisational multi-state programme that uses rugby to support social inclusion of 'at risk' or disadvantaged young people in Brazil and develop valuable skills such as leadership but also to develop the sport of rugby beyond a middle-class peripheral practice to one practised by more people across the country (see Hall and Reis, 2018). At the time, Try Rugby was the most intense rugby programme in Brazil. This programme provided an opportunity for sport scholars to examine the introduction, development and utilisation of rugby in peripheral nations as a social and self-development tool where there is an over-representation of football SfD programmes (see Schulenkorf, Sherry and Rowe, 2016). Moreover, Latin America (which accounts for approximately 3% of all SfD research) and in particular, Brazil was under-represented as a research site in SfD literature (Schulenkorf, Sherry and Rowe, 2016). But with the Rio 2016 Summer Olympics, Brazil became a focus of attention as a research site, while Try Rugby provided an opportunity to examine the impact rugby might have as an alternative sporting practice to football.

In the shadow of football: Rugby in Latin America

While most of Latin America had gained independence from European colonial rule by the early nineteenth century, the gradual adoption of European social conventions, such as codified sport (i.e. cricket, football and rugby), was used, ironically, to establish a sense of statehood to differentiate themselves from European nations as well as each other (Gaffney, 2008; Harris and Wise, 2011; Mangan, 2001). In particular, football became part of broader discourses across Latin American nations about statehood regarding their political and cultural identities (Bar-On, 1997). While the role of Britain in the development of modern sport in Latin America has been greater than any other nation (Arbena, 1995; Gutierrez, Antonio, Kater and de Almeida, 2017), the sport of rugby did not achieve similar cultural importance and continuity in its development in Latin America in the same way as football. It should be noted that Argentina maintained stronger trade links with Britain than other Latin American nations and is a place where rugby has a stronger presence (see Harris and Wise, 2011).

As football was popularised as a leisure activity, new clubs emerged across each country in Latin America, and leagues were established to accommodate and provide regulated and organised competition between clubs (Arbena, 1995). Football quickly became reified by governments, elite institutions and its regulatory bodies as a sport symbolising national unity among different races and classes, despite contemporary historical research suggesting it emphasised class and race division (Bar-On, 1997). By contrast, rugby and other British sports (such as cricket, cycling and tennis) in Latin America remained the practice of British communities and merchants in port cities (Mangan, 2001). While speculative, it is thought rugby's isolated practice, perhaps unintentionally, became seen by indigenous and other European migrants as a sport of middle-class snobbery (Bar-On, 1997). As such, most scholarly activity examining the political, sociological and historical influence of sport in Latin America tends to describe and emphasise the influence of football in Argentina.

Rugby in Brazil: a long past, a short history, but a bright future

Given the dominance of football in Latin America, rugby remained peripheral as a sporting practice. In Brazil, the sport was practised sporadically between British communities and as part of a few athletic clubs, where it was sometimes played in a festive-like manner as pre-match entertainment before a football game (Gutierrez et al., 2017). It was not until 1926, where we saw the first systematic attempt to establish rugby in Brazil. The first official match was played between São Paulo RFC and Santos RFC, and an annual organised competition, namely the Beilby-Alston Cup, was established between São Paulo RFC and Rio de Janeiro, Niteroi (incorporated into Rio Cricket and Athletic Association). Rugby went into a hiatus during Second World War, resuming after the war. The 1970s further institutionalised rugby as it integrated into university sporting practices attracting native Brazilians and rugby clubs relied less on foreign players (Portal do Rugby, 2011). However, the health of Brazilian rugby remained poor with a bleak outlook for survival, and by the mid-1990s, there were only approximately 800 players (Bath, 1997), despite Brazil becoming official members of the International Rugby Board in 1995.

In the last decade, Brazil has seen rugby expand rapidly as a consequence of several mass participation programmes (e.g. World Rugby's 'Get Into Rugby') introducing the sport into the school curriculum but also through increased funding of Brazilian rugby as part of World Rugby's Strategic Investment Programmes (International Rugby Board, 2013). Rugby was also commercialised in Spanish-speaking Latin America from 1999 through pay-per-view TV rights between the International Rugby Board and ESPN Latin America to show the Rugby World Cup from 1999 onwards (World Rugby, 2015a) and then ESPN Brazil from 2003 (World Rugby, 2015b). The Brazilian Rugby Confederation (Confederação Brasileira de Rugby; CBRu) attracted significant sponsorship deals in the following years. Moreover, since the inclusion of sevens as an Olympic sport, the Brazilian Olympic Committee invested £380,000 (equivalent to $500,000) in the Brazilian Rugby Confederation to develop its sevens programme (Stoney, 2012) in time for the Rio 2016 Summer Olympics.

Several development, investment and commercial factors converged in 2009 to improve rugby's visibility and participation, along with a change in sporting policy in 2010 to professionalise and invest in diversifying sporting habits in Brazil (Filho, Damiani and Fontana, 2018). This also appeared to have had a significant impact upon public

Table 7.1 Total number of Rugby players in Brazil, Argentina and Sudámerica Rugby[a]

	Brazil	Argentina	Sudámerica Rugby
2007	2,917	79,348	112,522
2008	3,532	91,459	127,289
2009	5,353	96,479	135,264
2010	10,130	102,789	150,086
2011	13,300	125,776	180,992
2012	13,012	121,162	176,640
2013	16,128	127,214	187,514
2014[b]	54,542 (5,403)	133,062 (56,998)	247,426 (78,110)
2015	109,000 (9,000)	134,563 (97,940)	336,221 (145,882)
2016	137,827 (16,659)	138,241 (105,151)	460,426 (165,567)
2017	185,155 (16,975)	143,770 (109,357)	545,301 (172,199)

a All figures compiled from World Rugby Annual Review data on total rugby players between 2007 and 2017.
b World Rugby began adding registered players to their figures indicated in parenthesis, but no further explanation is provided.

perception and player participation in rugby across the country as well. For example, within two years following the announcement rugby will return as a sport at the Rio 2016 Summer Olympics, a 2011 survey in Brazil found that rugby, while perceived as an unknown sporting practice, was the sport most likely to grow quickest alongside martial arts (Deloitte, 2011). In terms of participation in rugby, between 2007 and 2017, we see a significant increase in the number of participants (see Table 7.1). World Rugby's (2017) participation figures indicate that the total number of players practising rugby to be higher than Argentina. Subsequently, and regardless of the catalyst, rugby in Brazil has grown more in the last ten years than at any time in history.

Many Brazilian people have seen the introduction of rugby into Brazil's sporting practices as a recent one, and as such a sport without any established cultural or socio-historical 'baggage' around race, class or gender. It seems that rugby did not disappear as quickly as it was introduced towards the turn of the twentieth century, and the sport has maintained some continuity through a few clubs. While its early history might seem unremarkable, its achievement in remaining practised in Brazil is remarkable. The next section will now look at the area of SfD.

SfD and rugby

SfD is defined as a use of sport to foster positive influence on public health, the socialisation of children, youths and adults, the social inclusion of the disadvantaged, the economic development of regions and states and on fostering intercultural exchange and conflict resolution (Lyras and Welty Peachey, 2011). SfD programmes also vary in size, focus and type, but commonly all accept, often uncritically, the premise that sport 'is good for you' or 'sport works'. This has universal appeal to participants and organisations, and that social and economic development can be achieved through it (Coakley, 2015; Reis, Vieira and Sousa-Mast, 2016). While it is unclear how the association between sport and society came to be an important social convention, what is understood is that the value of sport in developing individuals, communities and societies, as multifaceted as it has become today, is fundamentally embedded in dogma and folk psychologies of Christian Socialism and the upper-class institutions of mid-nineteenth-century Britain (Kidd, 2008). That is, sport possesses inherent qualities that 'civilise' participants by teaching positive virtues and developing habits of good character and behaviour, such as self-restraint and control over emotions (see Dunning and Sheard, 1979). This is an association that Coakley (2015) terms, the 'Great Sports Myth'. Much of the academic literature, while producing some positive case studies, about the empowering influence sport can have on participants (e.g. Kay, 2009), have tended to criticise evidence for these underlying assumptions in SfD programmes as anecdotal (Harris and Adams, 2016; Schulenkorf, 2013), as well as making calls for more tailored implementation, monitoring and evaluation of SfD programmes given the varied approach that can be taken (Nols, Haudenhuyse and Theeboom, 2017).

While SfD programmes vary in focus (e.g. sport and disability, sport and gender), they can be distinguished by programme-specific outcomes (see Coalter, 2007; Kidd, 2008). As Hall and Reis (2018) summarise, *sport development* programme's raise a sport's profile, develop infrastructure for the sport to take place, enhance coaching and provide equipment to increase participation and develop sport-specific skills. In these programmes, the assumption remains that sport has inherent developmental properties for participants. *Sport plus* programmes (e.g. Mathare Youth Sport Association in Nairobi) are long-term projects that produce sustainable sport-focussed organisations and programmes where social benefits are a by-product of the programme (e.g. character development, leadership). *Plus sport* programmes use sport's popularity to attract young people to education programmes. These programmes are characterised by short-term outcomes (e.g. HIV/AIDs education and behaviour change; campaigns to challenge attitudes towards stigmatised groups) and are more important than the sport's long-term development. Here, sport plays a secondary role to the development outcomes. Boundaries between *sport plus* and *plus sport* programmes are not clear as outcomes are dictated by each organisation's values, visions and practices, as well as local needs. As Coalter (2010, p. 298) notes, 'sport is mostly a vitally important *necessary*, but not *sufficient* condition for the achievement of certain outcomes'. Embedded throughout these different models will be programmes that assume sport is an effective tool for the development of life skills, social knowledge, values and leadership qualities. As Hartmann and Kwauk (2011) summarise, this dominant vision embedded within SfD programmes is about resocialising youth, typically deemed 'at risk' to produce self-governing productive citizens that can contribute to society. This is a reproductive vision of established social relations. The transformation from potential 'deviants' to model citizens via the democratisation of sport to the masses, they are able to reconcile their social welfare debt and enhance their sense of social responsibility contributing to overall social and economic stability. Some *plus sport* programmes (e.g. UmRio rugby programme in Rio de Janeiro) offer *transformative vision* programmes to achieve social transformations by channelling the energies of sports towards more radical visions of development. Such interventionist programmes recognise that sporting practices are socially constructed and set within an equally constructed hierarchy of power, privilege and dominance. Sports in these programmes must be interwoven with other social change-orientated initiatives (e.g. education and health benefits). Thus, sport in this model becomes part of a broader strategy where participants are repositioned as active participants, changing their world and transforming society.

While SfD programmes do vary in sport, there is a dominance of football, and in a recent review by Schulenkorf, Sherry and Rowe (2016), football and general physical activity made up 60% of all SfD, while the remaining sport was dispersed across other popular sports, such as basketball, tennis and athletics. Rugby did not feature as a sport used by SfD programmes. As Darnell et al. (2016) further point out, an over reliance on football reflects a narrow perspective of sport and can promote traditional sporting values (e.g. competition and patriarchy) that are not typically part of SfD assumptions as described above. Moreover, Darnell et al. (2016) argue that because SfD programmes are not necessarily apolitical and value free, using football as the main choice of development activity might constitute a form of cultural hegemony by positioning football organisations as key stakeholders in SfD activity, while also promoting traditional sporting (and masculine) values not typically associated with SfD, such as competition, dominance and patriarchy.

Rugby offers an alternative vehicle for development to football. Given its format as a competitive team sport, it is hard to fully comprehend how dissimilar it can be to the structures found in football. For example, rugby still promotes competition and other sporting traditions found in football, such as dominance and patriarchy that are counter to the SfD assumptions of inclusivity (see Darnell et al., 2016). While many would encourage the use of diversifying the opportunities for participants to engage with different sports, the use of traditional popular European team focussed sport reproduce and assumed the same 'sport works' narrative in development contexts. In short, rugby will still offer itself as a sport that offers opportunity for development because it speaks a 'universal language' of inclusivity, of which is shared with football. It will still be used as a 'pacifying' experience for youth prone to negative coercion and for instilling morals and values in an attempt to produce a resilient youth in the face of marginalisation (Darnell et al., 2016). Moreover, rugby, like football, implements hierarchical and categorised ability (e.g. by gender) and is unlikely to lead to egalitarian and inclusive outcomes in the same way that football might not (Darnell et al., 2016). While these are not inherently negative, the 'sport works' narrative is embedded within rugby. This is further highlighted in World Rugby's values incorporated into their charter (World Rugby, 2009). These values of integrity, passion, solidarity, discipline and respect are the defining character-building characteristics of rugby and aim to maintain rugby's 'unique' character. However, it is assumed that just by playing rugby, these values will be instilled in its participants, and it is unclear how this is made possible other than through rugby ambassadors.

Growing rugby in Brazil: the case of Try Rugby in Brazil

As part of our interest in examining rugby's development in Brazil, several field trips were made to Brazil during 2015. Specifically, Premiership Rugby's Try Rugby programme was examined in two states: São Paulo and Rio de Janeiro. Leveraging rugby's inclusion into the Rio 2016 Olympics, Premiership Rugby in England, independent of World Rugby and the CBRu, established the Try Rugby grassroots project. Try Rugby was run in conjunction with the British Council and Social Service for Industry in Schools (SESI), a common SfD model in Brazil (see Reis, Vieira and Sousa-Mast, 2016). At a reported cost of £500,000 (Stoney, 2012), the project was expected to last four years (2012–2016, but extended until 2017) with a legacy of long-term sustainable practice of rugby (through training school coaches) and a host of other social and health benefits. Like other SfD programmes, the objectives of Try Rugby attempted to utilise the sport as a social development tool in low-income communities across different states in Brazil. It was also the most ambitious programme in Brazil attempting the greatest public reach and expansion of the sport of rugby, encouraging participants to live more active and healthy lifestyles.

While it was primarily a *sport development* programme, the programme made claims that it would provide social benefits beyond the sport in line with *sport plus* models. For example, in their mission statement, Premiership Rugby claimed that rugby would be a tool to support the social inclusion of 'at risk' or disadvantaged young people in Brazil and develop valuable skills such as leadership (Premiership Rugby, 2016). As such, the programme was assuming participants, in the absence of any formal training by programme leaders, did not have leadership skills or they, at best, needed developing in a manner described in the dominant vision of SfD (see Hartmann and Kwauk, 2011). By 2014, the programme had introduced rugby to 24 sites across the states of Minas Gerais, Santa Catarina and São Paulo. By its fourth year in 2016, the programme had reached 18,000 participants every week, nearly 70,000 individuals through various workshops, and over 350 volunteers and teachers were trained to deliver tag rugby and referee rugby games (Premiership Rugby, 2016). Since the research visit to Brazil, the project has expanded into Colombia and the United States.

During the field trip, data was collected from media documents. Coaches and managers, 'street bureaucrats', were interviewed (Harris and Adams, 2016) to understand their motivations and assumptions for how the programme is developing not only rugby but also its participants in the manner described by their mission statements and the attributes prescribed in World Rugby's charter. Interviews were anchored around the following three core themes: (1) What is unique about sport, and in particular rugby, as a social and development activity? (2) How and why does rugby 'transform' individual participants and communities? and (3) To what extent are such personal and social transformations evidenced in achieving the programmes outcomes? To structure the data, thematic analysis (Braun and Clarke, 2006) was used to help identify and interpret key features and patterns in the discourse guided by the research questions.

Following the analysis, two dominant themes were identified. The findings suggested tensions between the partner organisations concerning promoting the social development outcomes (e.g. *plus sport*) or promoting rugby and its values (e.g. *sport development*). Rugby was reified as a character development tool and a sport that 'works' due to its unique characteristics, often juxtaposed by discussing its value relative to football. Rugby was a vehicle for building discipline, as well as developing 'soft' skills to use in everyday life. For example, the whistle was an important prop for coaches when initially introducing new participants to rugby. During these initial stages some coaches drew comparisons between rugby and football player's respect towards a referee and his whistle. The intentions of Try Rugby are, therefore, expected to provide participants with a 'moral compass' and enable them to become responsible citizens. Such an emphasis confirms Hartmann and Kwauk's (2011) criticism of many SfD programmes reproducing *Dominant Vision* discourses where programmes attempt to recalibrate youth (whether it is the main priority or not) to enhance their sense of self and reconcile an economic debt to society in future.

In the second theme identified, it became clearer that the priorities of the programme were to develop rugby's growth and acceptance in Brazil before the Rio 2016 Olympics. In general, this theme focused on positive language around diversifying sporting practices in Brazil through rugby. Understandably, the Olympics provided an opportunity to justify promoting Premiership Rugby and its goals (raise awareness of the sport of rugby) in Brazil. While the programme did not require a mega-event to facilitate social change, it is likely that its leveraging of the Rio 2016 Olympics facilitated its legitimacy as a successful and attractive project relative to another football-orientated programme. It also provided the necessary propulsion to expand the programme into other states in Brazil.

Indeed, managers in the collaborative organisations (British Council and SESI) emphasised offering an alternative sport away from football and enriching their education through something 'different'. Interviews with the coaches highlight that there are no structured systems for developing social change other than a belief system that learning rugby-specific skills and being a good role model will produce the change identified in the programme outcomes. Furthermore, the coaches use their position as surrogate role models to instil values of rugby and life. Such insight implies a sense of legitimate authority between the participants and coaches who impart the knowledge of how to live a disciplined, integral and valuable life to those disadvantaged members of society who may need to more fully understand discipline and how to behave appropriately.

Despite the social development and 'sport works' assumptions within the Try Rugby programme, it was a prototypical dominant vision, and specifically *sport development* (Kidd, 2008) and *sport plus*

(Coalter, 2007). All organisations involved in the project had a shared conceptual basis for the project, namely that rugby will have a positive effect on participants, that 'sport is good'. Evidence from interviews demonstrated that for coaches, part of their aim was to 'recalibrate' the participants using the core values of rugby. Any perceived transformations were solely left to coaches delivering sport-specific skills and teaching the values of rugby to instil the appropriate character, mind and skill set that are popular in positive youth development literature. The research suggests that the coaches are the most important asset in providing any knowledge transfer regarding sport-specific life skills and that these are structured around vague terminology and analogies. Given that the practice of sport exists within a commodified global sports order, the evidence suggests that Try Rugby is encouraging a reproduction of traditional SfD structures and hierarchies rather than attempting a meaningful and sustainable social transformation.

Overall, utilising coaches as a data source showed that the dominant 'sport works' repertoires also exist within a rugby context, and with the exception of impressive reach and participation numbers across Brazil, the evidence available of any social or behaviour change did not appear. As our study shows, the sport works discourse is dominant, and it is unclear how calls for understanding voices of coaches (see also, Harris and Adams, 2016) in novel research sites (like Brazil) will show anything beyond the prevailing dominant discourse without a proper design and implementation of these programmes to target and develop the 'life skills' many claim to be teaching. As we have noted elsewhere, the programme is successful in achieving mass participation, while upholding populist mantra about sport's ability to transform individuals and communities without supporting its broader social change outcomes (Hall and Reis, 2018). Significantly, it also reinforces a dominant vision for SfD programmes without critically reflecting upon their own practices and the consequences of such reproduction. As noted by Kidd (2008), the positive language used in SfD programmes now support a self-confirming industry based around sport as a legitimate solution to social problems.

The future of rugby in Brazil

The brief overview provided above has shown that with investment, rugby in a peripheral nation emerged from the brink of extinction to a rapidly growing sport with a bright future. In the coming years, World Rugby will release new figures about the uptake in the sport in Brazil. Should participation numbers continue to increase, future directions should focus on the emergence of a rugby culture beyond Rio 2016 and how the sport will become self-sustaining following the initial development funds and participation programmes. It is also important to maintain continuity in examining the legacies of each source of development following the Rio 2016 Summer Olympics. For example, the Try Rugby programme has come to an end, but we know nothing about how the sustainable practice of rugby was maintained in the schools in which they were embedded. Given the reach they achieved during their programme, it would be difficult for the sport to maintain its positive trajectory if the interest in rugby was not fostered. However, as rugby continues its expansion into peripheral nations, its growth has also attracted more female players than ever before, where nearly 30% of all rugby players in 2017 across the world are female (Wigmore, 2018). The success of the Brazilian Women's Sevens team is likely to be an important catalyst for growing the image of rugby as an inclusive sport in Brazil, but perhaps more importantly for Brazil as a sport that relies less upon the dominant eight rugby nations for funding and have a far stronger voice in shaping and recalibrating contemporary rugby practices. As Wigmore (2018) writes, 'the future of rugby union is bright, global, but female', and perhaps nowhere is this currently more pronounced than in Brazil. Finally, if rugby wishes to continue to develop its alternative values to football, then like many criticisms of SfD programmes and approaches, clear structures from implementation and evaluation are required to fully articulate and evidence the added value rugby can bring to its participants' lives beyond the rugby field rather than rely on the standardised rhetoric of 'Sport Works' (Coakley, 2015; Harris and Adams, 2016).

References

Arbena, J. L. (1995). Nationalism and sport in Latin America, 1850–1990: The paradox of promoting and performing 'European' sports. *The International Journal of the History of Sport*, 12(2), 220–238.

Bath, R. (1997). *The complete book of Rugby*. Sevenoaks: Dubai.

Bar-On, T. (1997). The ambiguities of football, politics, culture, and social transformation in Latin America. *Sociological Research Online*, 2(4). Available at www.socresonline.org.uk/2/4/2.html

Braun, V., and Clarke, V. (2006). Using thematic analysis in psychology. *Qualitative Research in Psychology*, 3(2), 77–101.

Coakley, J. (2015). Assessing the sociology of sport: On cultural sensibilities and the great sport myth. *International Review for the Sociology of Sport*, 50(4–5), 402–406.

Coalter, F. (2007). *A wider social role for sport: Who's keeping the score?* London: Routledge.

Coalter, F. (2010). The politics of sport-for-development: Limited focus programmes and broad gauge problems? *International Review for the Sociology of Sport*, 45(3), 295–314.

Deloitte (2011). Muito Além do Futebol – Estudo sobre esportes no Brasil. Available at www.deloitte.com.br/Comunicados/ReleasePesquisaEsportes.pdf

Darnell, S., Chawansky, M., Marchesseault, D., Holmes, M., and Hayhurst, L. (2016). The state of play: Critical sociological insights into recent sport for development and peace research. *International Review for the Sociology of Sport*, 53(2), 1–19.

Dunning, E., and Sheard, K. (1979). *Barbarians, gentlemen and players: A sociological study of the development of rugby football.* Oxford: Martin Robertson.

Filho, A., Damiani, C., and Fontana, P. (2018). Sports mega-events in Brazil: An account of the Brazilian government's actions. *Acta Universitatis Carolinae: Kinanthropologica*, 54(1), 28–40.

Gaffney, C. (2008). *Temples of the earthbound gods: Stadiums in the cultural landscapes of Rio de Janeiro and Buenos Aires.* Austin: University of Texas Press.

Gutierrez, D., Antonio, V., Kater, T., and de Almeida, M. (2017). Um estudo sobre a introdução e institucionalização do rugby no Brasil 1891–1940. *Journal of Physical Education*, 28(1), 2841.

Hartmann, D., and Kwauk, C. (2011). Sport and development: An overview, critique, and reconstruction. *Journal of Sport & Social Issues*, 35(3), 284–305.

Hall, G., and Reis, A. (2018). A case study of sport for development in Brazil. *Bulletin of Latin American Research*. Available at doi:10.1111/blar.12921

Harris, J., and Wise, N. (2011). Geographies of scale in international rugby union. *Geographical Research*, 49(4), 375–383.

Harris, K., and Adams, A. (2016). Power and discourse in the politics of evidence in sport for development. *Sport Management Review*, 19, 97–106.

International Rugby Board (2013). Year in review. Available at www.world.rugby/documents/annual-reports?lang=en

Kay, T. (2009). Developing through sport: Evidencing sport impacts on young people. *Sport in Society*, 12(9), 1177–1191.

Kidd, B. (2008). A new social movement: Sport for development and peace. *Sport in Society*, 11(4), 370–380.

Lyras, A., and Welty Peachey, J. (2011). Integrating sport-for-development theory and praxis. *Sport Management Review*, 14(4), 311–326.

Mangan, J. A. (2001). The early evolution of modern sport in Latin America: A mainly English middle-class inspiration? *The International Journal of the History of Sport*, 18(3), 9–42.

Nols, Z., Haudenhuyse, R., and Theeboom, M. (2017). Urban sport-for-development initiatives and young people in socially vulnerable situations: Investigating the 'deficit model'. *Social Inclusion*, 5(2), 210–222.
Portal do Rugby (2011). History of rugby. Available at www.portaldorugby.com.br/entenda-o-rugby/historia-do-rugby
Premiership Rugby (2016). *Online interview*. Available at http://exeterchiefs.co.uk/news/skys-the-limit-for-try-rugby-programme/
Reis, A., Vieira, M., and Sousa-Mast, F. (2016). Sport for development in developing countries: The case of the Vilas Olímpicas do Rio de Janeiro. *Sport Management Review*, 19(2), 107–119.
Schulenkorf, N. (2013). Sport for development events and social capital building: A critical analysis of experiences from Sri Lanka. *Journal of Sport for Development*, 1(1), 25–36.
Schulenkorf, N., Sherry, E., and Rowe, K. (2016). Sport for development: An integrated literature review. *Journal of Sport Management*, 30(1), 22–39.
Stoney, E. (2012). Soccer-crazy Brazil opening its arms to rugby. *The New York Times*, Available at https://nyti.ms/RGsfji
Wigmore, T. (2018). The future of rugby union is bright, global, and female. *iNews*, Available at https://inews.co.uk/sport/rugby-union/rugby-union-global-shift-women/
World Rugby (2009). Laws of the game. Available at https://laws.worldrugby.org/?charter=all&language=EN
World Rugby (2015a). ESPN Latin America and ESPN Brazil join RWC broadcast family. Available at www.rugbyworldcup.com/news/65936?lang=en
World Rugby (2015b). Year in review. Available at www.world.rugby/documents/annual-reports?lang=en
World Rugby (2017). Year review. Available at www.world.rugby/documents/annual-reports?lang=en

8 Rugby beyond the core in Africa

Nicholas Wise

Introduction

Business Focus Reporter (2018) headlines 'Africa is among the fastest-growing rugby fan-bases with 32.7m'. This chapter will focus on the growth and expansion of different versions of rugby in Africa. South Africa is one of the eight foundation nations of the sport's governing body and is the only country on the continent to excel internationally.

To take a step back and consider some historical context of sport/rugby in Africa, we need to consider sport and geographical imaginations. In many instances, the globally recognised sports of today that were introduced to Africa during the nineteenth century were inherently linked to colonialism, based on what Odendaal (1990) refers to as 'microcosms' to guide colonial society and social structures (see also, Darby, 2002). Sport became embedded in the social fabric of nations, and even led to division, or were signifiers of race and class, as was the case in South Africa based on participation in sports such as rugby and association football (see Crawford, 1999). It is beyond the scope of this chapter to detail sociological connotations surrounding sport and social issues, but sport offers much insight into how we imagine and perceive nations, sporting culture and national identity (see Bale and Sang, 1996). Research on sport and geographical imaginations has outlined the importance of a geographical approach to the study of sport (e.g. Bale, 2003; Wise, 2015). Bale (2003) dedicated an entire chapter to imaginative geographies in his book because our cognitive associations often link certain sports with particular places. Wise (2015, p. 147) noted that 'rugby is popular in south Wales, Australian rules football is extremely popular in the greater Melbourne area and the Gaelic Games symbolize Irish heritage and nationalism'.

Based on colonial legacies, football, cricket and rugby are considered the three most widely played sports where nations compete globally

(Sikes, 2018). While rugby is played across the continent of Africa, the imagination of the sport, its popular presence and the game's attention is directed to South Africa. A cursory Google search for sport and rugby in Africa directs us to South African rugby or images of the Springboks. The same is true when searching for academic literature on rugby in Africa where these yield results of South Africa, with little scholarly discussion disseminated among other countries in such a vast continent (discussed with references below). Popular imaginations of sport in Africa are directed to South Africa often because they are the only nation in Africa to host a mega-sporting event – the 2010 FIFA World Cup, and previously the 1995 Rugby World Cup (RWC). They were arguably the only sub-Saharan country with the economic capability to host the mega-event (Cornelisen, 2007); moreover, South Africa is a globally recognised emerging economy (or a BRICS nation, referring to Brazil, Russia, India, China and South Africa). The 2010 FIFA World Cup was considered 'Africa's World Cup', or as Bolsmann (2011) described, an event with Pan-Africanist rhetoric and imagery, to emphasise modernity. Six African nations (Algeria, Cameroon, Ghana, Ivory Coast, Nigeria and South Africa) competed in the event, and much attention was drawn to Ghana who made it the farthest in the competition of all the African nations (to the quarter-finals). It must also be noted that Morocco have previously bid to host the FIFA World Cup.

Imaginations of Africa also differ geographically as there are significant cultural differences between nations in the north of the continent and sub-Saharan African nations. Saying this, in World Geography text books, Africa is split into two major world regions with northern African nations regionally considered Middle East and North Africa (or North Africa and Southwest Asia), and sub-Saharan Africa having its own chapter – with the Sahara as the spatial/cultural divide. For the purpose of this chapter, Africa is considered physiographically as a continent of 54 countries according to the United Nations (including island nations off the coast of the continental land mass).

Similar to Chapter 2 on Argentina, building on conceptual understandings by Harris and Wise (2011), notions of core and periphery are discussed again in this chapter to look at the positioning of key countries in Africa as the sport gains popularity. Next, I discuss the presence of African nations in the RWC. The following section considers Rugby in Africa and World Rugby's continental strategy. This section goes beyond the international discussion in the previous section to look at continental competition and the lack of development and investment in women's rugby. Then, this chapter will consider the sevens version of the game in Africa as an important driver of rugby in the area. The final section brings this chapter together by looking at the game's development and future in Africa.

Presence beyond South Africa in the RWC

To start the evaluation of rugby in Africa, it is important to first consider the presence of African nations in the RWC. South Africa Men's won the 1995 and 2007 RWCs, but the South Africa Women's best performance to date is tenth place. This section is concerned with other African nations to compete in the RWC.

By considering African nations in international competition, this positions them in the rugby landscape of cores and peripheries. Acknowledging the nations that have entered the top flight of international competition show where the sport may be most developed; it also challenges us to acknowledge why particular nations are able to compete, while others are still seeing the sport develop. In Africa, Ivory Coast, Namibia and Zimbabwe are the only nations other than South Africa to compete in the RWC to date (see Wise, 2017). While these four nations have presence in the RWC, they have not been regular competitors. South Africa, for instance, was banned from participating in the 1987 and 1991 RWCs because of pro-Apartheid policies, but as the political landscape in the country changed in the early-1990s South Africa would host (and win) the 1995 event (and has since competed in all RWCs). The other three African countries to complete in the RWC are Zimbabwe (in 1987 and 1991), Ivory Coast (in 1995) and Namibia (in 1999, 2003, 2007, 2011 and 2015 and have also qualified for 2019). Based on the qualification of an African nation, it is only one country (in addition to South Africa since 1995) that will qualify. If another country from Africa were to qualify, they need to win a Repechage playoff. Given the strict eligibility requirements to enter the RWC competition, we see from 1987 to 2019, these three countries have never competed against each other. For each event they were the sole African nation able to qualify for the RWC (based on number of countries per region who are able to enter the competition). Kenya did have the chance to qualify for Japan 2019 but did not succeed during Repechage qualification in 2018.

Namibia has never won a match in a RWC competition, but they are clearly the top rugby union team in Africa based on Gold Cup performance. At the 2015 RWC, Namibia lost to Georgia by one point. This shows that there is a vast difference in competition at the African continental level compared to the wider international level. From a core and periphery standpoint, this shows how peripheral the development of African rugby is (beyond South Africa) when performing at the elite level. Nevertheless, in African competition, Namibia clearly stands out going undefeated in the last two Africa Gold Cup competitions. The balance, therefore, is finding that middle ground as how to advance African countries in international competition outside continental competition. Ivory Coast and Zimbabwe during their appearances in the RWC have also failed to win a match. In 1995, Ivory Coast was defeated 89-0 by Scotland in a pool stage match. Placing these three African countries in global perspective, Wise (2017) positioned them on the boundary of Tier 2 and Tier 3 nations in his core/periphery model solely because they have RWC experience.

Looking at the Women's RWC, the competition is also very limited in terms of entry. Only 12 teams compete in the competition, and the South African's women's team has been the only African nation to qualify (in 2006, 2010 and 2014). Despite qualification, they have only been able to reach as high as tenth place in the competition. This shows a clear lack of development in the Women's version of the game in Africa, as per some of the points noted in the next section, but there is much more focus on the sevens version of the game discussed later in this chapter. Rugby Afrique (2019b) has organised a continent-wide celebration of women's rugby, noting May as the month of Women's rugby in Africa. The 2018 Sevens event was held in Gaborone, Botswana.

Rugby in Africa and World Rugby's continental strategy

Rugby has a long-standing tradition in Africa, with the game being fairly widespread across the continent. There have been thorough analyses of sport and Africa focusing on football (see Alegi, 2010), but such work on Africa and rugby is still needed. However, a wide range of academic literature on rugby and Africa over the past few decades, from social science perspectives, is dominated by work focusing on South Africa (e.g. Allen, 2014; Black and Nauright, 1988; Grundlingh, 2015; Steenveld and Strelitz, 1998; Van Der Merwe, 2007). Some work has assessed rugby and sport science, but little work has looked at rugby from a social sciences perspective in Africa beyond research on South Africa. For example, research that has looked at the role of rugby other countries in Africa tend to focus on grassroots development or sociological dilemmas, such as sport and racial division in Zimbabwe (Novak, 2012), human resources and strategy implications (Obomate, 2016) and some links to the role of rugby in postcolonial Uganda (Chappell, 2008).

94 *Nicholas Wise*

Part of the struggle with rugby in Africa from a sociological standpoint is the game's association with racial and class divides. It has long been observed in the literature on rugby's diffusion into Africa from colonialisation that the sport has been linked to racial divide. For instance, during Apartheid, rugby was seen as a sport associated with the white upper class and football was played predominantly by the black population (see Crawford, 1999). This was depicted in the film *Invictus* to show the sport and race divide and the role of Nelson Mandela in striving for unity to create opportunities for people off all races and classes in South Africa (see Wise, 2014). While divisions persist in South Africa, it was not until 2018 that the country appointed their first black captain, Siya Kolisi, for full test matches (Bull, 2018). Racial quotas are common in South African sport representation, not only in rugby but also netball, athletics and cricket. Bull (2018) highlights 'racial quotas in the Springbok selection process are still a regular subject of rancour but Kolisi is living proof of their ongoing validity and usefulness'. The other challenge is speaking back to how South African rugby dominates the discussion of sports sociology, but little has been done to position the game and assess the growth and development of the sport outside of South Africa. Rugby Afrique (2019a) note:

> development is the key word. But what does it really mean to develop? Today proud of our 38 member unions, we wish to grow the game beyond capital cities, big towns and major clubs. Our work on the field aims at pricking the curiosity of young people and others to introduce them to a sport too often victim of misconceptions.

While development is the focus on growing the game in Africa, people across the continent struggle with misconceptions of how the sport is viewed (Rugby Afrique, 2019a). Many view rugby as a violent sport, so the governing body struggles with issues of the game's image and is reaching out to youth to develop the sport and highlight the importance of teambuilding and leadership skills (Rugby Afrique, 2019a).

Today, there is a need to consider the development of the sport and the positioning of the game based on the role and performance of other countries, along with consideration of different versions of the game such as sevens with has the potential to influence the growth of rugby in Africa. Currently in Africa, there are 38 registered member unions registered with Rugby Afrique (the sports continental governing body) and World Rugby. The 38-member unions can be seen on the map in Figure 8.1, detailing the number of registered players and each member union's World Rugby ranking. One of the challenges is

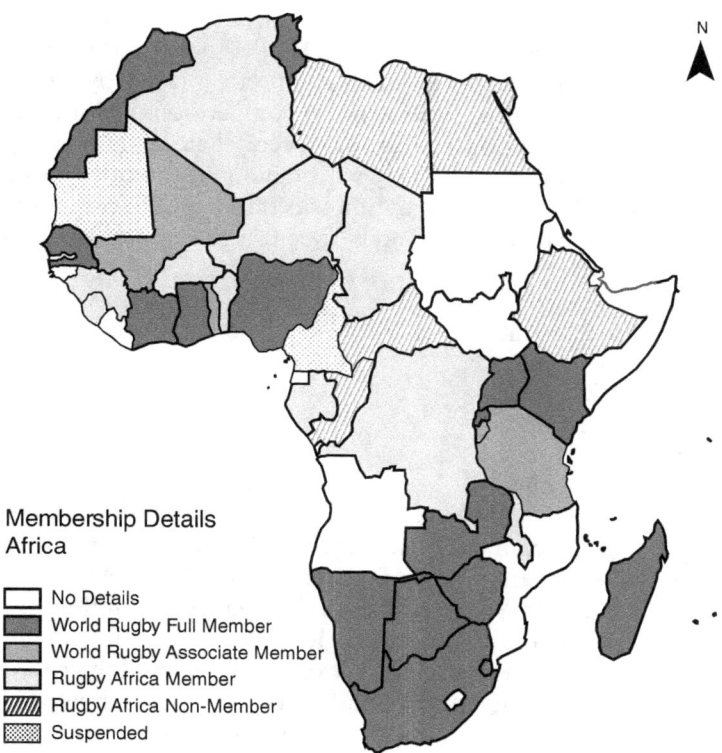

Figure 8.1 Africa's member unions.
Note: Cape Verde is not visible on this map but they are listed as a Rugby Africa Non-Member.

much more attention is given to the men's versions of rugby in Africa, so World Rugby and Rugby Afrique are looking at ways to develop the women's game. In 2018, a leadership and strategy forum on women's rugby was held in Gaborone, Botswana, a week before the women's Sevens tournament took place in the same city (CNBCAfrica, 2018). Rugby Afrique (2019b) speaks about the challenges around developing the sport that link to religion, public opinion and cultural backgrounds. The main concern that Rugby Afrique (2019b) acknowledges is 'the lack of women in the union's leadership and the lack of players and infrastructure [... as women] seldom have a female role model to look up to in the world of rugby', which is what the leadership forum aimed to address and action with the assistance of World Rugby.

One way that Rugby Afrique is seeking to establish an international continental competition is through a series of events: Gold Cup, Silver Cup and Bronze Cup. While there are attempts to develop the women's game, these events are played by the men's national teams. The organisation of the competitions is similar to the Six Nations competition in Europe, where each country competes in five matches, and the country with the highest number of points wins the cup. The 2018 competition was important because it was a RWC qualifier competition, held between June and August, with the following result:

1. Namibia (25 points)
2. Kenya (17 points)
3. Uganda (9 points)
4. Tunisia (9 points)
5. Zimbabwe (8 points)
6. Morocco (3 points)

In an attempt to keep the competition inclusive to allow nations to compete at the highest level in Africa, there is a relegation process that means the team with the fewest points will compete the following year in the Silver Cup and the top-performing Silver Cup team will join the Gold Cup. However, in 2019 to expand the event, they will move to an eight-nation competition. South Africa has not competed in the competition because they play in The Rugby Championship.

The current fixture has been played over the past two years in 2017 and 2018, and the results of the fixtures are displayed in Table 8.1. Prior to 2017, nations competed at three levels, displayed as 1A, 1B and 1C. From Table 8.1, we see that the top-five teams have remained the same, but allowing for Morocco to compete in the Gold Cup in 2018 allows for different teams to compete to alter the competition each year. Algeria enters the Gold Cup in 2019 and Namibia clearly stands out as the strongest team (outside South Africa) based on their performance standing in Table 8.1. Winning the Gold Cup in 2018 allowed Namibia to qualify for the 2019 RWC. Because Kenya was the 2018 Gold Cup runner-up, they were invited to a Repechage qualification to compete against Canada, Germany and Hong Kong for a final spot in the 2019 RWC. Canada won the Repechage qualification. Outside South Africa, Namibia is clearly the second strongest rugby union nation, going undefeated in Gold Cup competition in 2017 and 2018. The 2019 Gold Cup will move to an eight-team competition, so

Rugby beyond the core in Africa 97

Table 8.1 Africa Cup result fixtures in 2015 and 2016; Gold Cup, Silver Cup and Bronze Cup result fixtures in 2017 and 2018

2015		
Division 1A	Division 1B	Division 1C
1 Namibia	Uganda (advance-1A)	Zambia (advance-1B)
2 Zimbabwe	Madagascar	Nigeria
3 Kenya	Senegal	Zimbabwe
4 Tunisia (relegated)	Ivory Coast	Morocco (did not compete)
5	Botswana	
6	Mauritius (relegated)	
2016		
Division 1A	Division 1B	Division 1C
1 Namibia	Tunisia (advance-Gold)	Morocco (advance-Silver)
2 Kenya	Senegal (advance-Gold)	Nigeria
3 Uganda	Madagascar	Mauritius
4 Zimbabwe	Ivory Coast	
5	Botswana	
6	Zambia (relegated)	
2017		
Gold Cup	Silver Cup	Bronze Cup
1 Namibia	Morocco (advance-Gold)	Algeria (advance-Silver)
2 Kenya	Ivory Coast	Zambia (advance-Silver)
3 Uganda	Madagascar	Rwanda
4 Tunisia	Botswana	Mauritius
5 Zimbabwe		Nigeria (withdrew)
6 Senegal (relegated)		Cameroon (suspended)
2018		
Gold Cup	Silver Cup	Bronze Cup
1 Namibia (qualify-2019 RWC)	Algeria (advance-Gold)	Ghana
2 Kenya	Zambia (advance-Gold)	Mauritius
3 Uganda	Madagascar	Rwanda
4 Tunisia	Ivory Coast	Lesotho
5 Zimbabwe	Senegal	
6 Morocco	Botswana	

Source: Rugby Afrique (2018).

Morocco avoids relegation and Algeria and Zambia advance to the Gold Cup (see Nabiswa, 2018).

If we are to look at regional scales and develop a core and periphery module, adopting a similar framework to Wise (2017), we could position Namibia as a core African rugby playing nation given their success in the Gold Cup and regular presence in the RWC. Zimbabwe and Ivory Coast could be considered part of the emerging core, as they both have previous RWC experiences. However, in recent years, Zimbabwe competed in the Africa Gold Cup but Ivory Coast in the Africa Silver Cup, so this shows that the development in the game in Ivory Coast has not advanced since they competed at the 1995 RWC.

Africa Rugby Sevens

While there were a few nations that have been recognised as internationally competitive, Kwoba (2018) notes sevens as the future of rugby in Africa, suggesting 'teams that have developed tremendously in the shorter version of the sport, Uganda, Tunisia, Morocco, Zimbabwe and Namibia saying they are just a step from crashing the party of world elite Sevens rugby'. Concerning women's rugby in Africa, developing a 15-a-side competition was not possible so a sevens competition was organised and has been competed yearly since 2013 – dominated by South Africa and Kenya.

The return of rugby to the Olympic Games is also important to note here as Rio 2016 represented a turning point for the sport, and especially as this shorter version of the game is growing in popularity across Africa, it gave nations the chance to compete in a widely publicised event. South Africa and Kenya qualified for the men's event and only Kenya qualified for the women's event. With Kenya as the only nation to qualify both a women's and a men's team, this suggests Kenya has an opportunity to shine on the international rugby sevens stage. Although both Kenya's teams did not perform particularly well, their inclusion helps enhance the sport's domestic popularity.

The RWC Sevens is another international competition that Africa have representation in Table 8.2. In rugby sevens events, six different nations from Africa competed in the men's event, and three nations in three women's events. For Uganda, 2009 was the first time the nation competed in any international rugby event. As common in international rugby competition, South Africa has competed in all men's/women's events and Kenya and Zimbabwe men's teams each competed in five events. Another international competition, the World Rugby Sevens Series, has been held annually since the 1999–2000 season. This competition has seen South Africa men place in the top six in each event. Kenya men's saw success placing fifth in 2012–2013. Morocco,

Table 8.2 African nations finishing place in the Women's and Men's Rugby World Cup Sevens competition

	1993	1997	2001	2005	2009	2013	2018
Women							
South Africa					3	13	14
Tunisia						13	
Uganda					13		
Men							
Kenya			19	19	3	4	16
Namibia	21	21					
South Africa	5	2	5	5	5	5	3
Tunisia				13	13	21	
Uganda							19
Zimbabwe		21	21		17	13	23

Source: Rugby Afrique.

Namibia, Tunisia, Uganda and Zimbabwe round out the seven African nations that have competed in the series. While Namibia stood out as the top African nation continentally, Kenya stands out in the sevens version of the game (and are 1 of 15 core nations that are invited to all ten events). The women's Sevens Series since 2012–2013 has only seen three African nations compete, Kenya, South Africa and Tunisia, and no African nation has finished in the top six.

Looking at continental competition to conclude this section, Africa Sevens rugby has a strong foundation over the past 20 years, with a men's tournament since 2000 and a women's tournament since 2008. Table 8.3 shows women's/men's Africa Sevens results since becoming an annual competition. Beyond South Africa, the Kenyan women's team stands out having been either the winner or runner-up in the past five years. In the men's competition, Kenya does stand out, but Uganda and Zimbabwe have also seen success since Africa Sevens became an annual competition. The challenge is getting more nations to compete; women's have seen 12 nations and men's 15 nations. With 38 unions registered with World Rugby in Africa, there is still room for development from the perspective of continental competition. Many countries who are active in African competition are peripheral from an international standpoint, the registered unions that do not compete in regular African competitions are situated further in the periphery.

Table 8.3 Africa Women's and Men's Sevens results since becoming an annual competition

Year	Host	1st place	2nd place	3rd place	4th place	Other nations
Women's						
2013	Tunisia	South Africa	Tunisia	Uganda	Kenya	Senegal, Zimbabwe
2014	Kenya	South Africa	Kenya	Tunisia	Zimbabwe	Madagascar, Namibia, Senegal, Uganda
2015	South Africa	South Africa	Kenya	Tunisia	Zimbabwe	Botswana, Madagascar, Namibia, Senegal, Uganda, Zambia
2016	Zimbabwe	South Africa	Kenya	Zimbabwe	Uganda	Madagascar, Namibia, Senegal, Tunisia
2017	Tunisia	South Africa	Kenya	Tunisia	Uganda	Madagascar, Morocco, Senegal, Zimbabwe
2018	Botswana	Kenya	Uganda	Tunisia	Madagascar	Mauritius, Morocco, Senegal, Zambia, Zimbabwe
Men's						
2013	Kenya	Kenya	Zimbabwe	Details not available	Details not available	Ivory Coast, Kenya B, Madagascar, Morocco, Namibia, Nigeria, Senegal, Tunisia, Uganda, Zambia
2014	Zimbabwe	South Africa	Kenya	Zimbabwe	Tunisia	Full list of teams in the competition not found
2015	South Africa	Kenya	Zimbabwe	Morocco	Tunisia	Botswana, Madagascar, Mauritius, Namibia, Nigeria, Senegal, Uganda, Zambia
2016	Kenya	Uganda	Namibia	Kenya	Madagascar	Botswana, Mauritius, Morocco, Nigeria, Senegal, Tunisia, Zambia, Zimbabwe
2017	Uganda	Uganda	Zimbabwe	Madagascar	Zambia	Botswana, Ghana, Mauritius, Morocco, Senegal, Tunisia
2018	Tunisia	Zimbabwe	Kenya	Uganda	Madagascar	Botswana, Ghana, Mauritius, Morocco, Namibia, Senegal, Tunisia, Zambia

Source: Rugby Afrique.

Try for the future, ruck the past

In previous work on the RWC, I addressed the need to focus on new directions, opposed to more of the same (see Wise, 2017). Going beyond more of the same is the focus of the 2019 RWC being hosted in Japan and also the focus of this collection. There is 'Get into Rugby', which is aimed at getting children to participate in the sport – and is linked to the promotion of women's rugby as well. The programme has seen 'more than 400,000 participants in 2017, and 40 per cent being women' (Kwoba, 2018).

For Africa, it is about framing and positioning a new vision of rugby. One approach would be to focus on grassroots development of rugby as key to the further growth of the sport, building on work discussed in Chapter 7 by Gareth Hall and Arianne Reis. But Africa is a very different place, and Calderisi (2006) argued that development and planning in Africa is not a matter of taking, so-called best practices from elsewhere to come up with solutions – he suggested the best plan for development in Africa is actually to have 'no plan'. However, sport governing bodies do not approach participation and growth to achieve new contracts and attract media rights in this way. But while World Rugby has a strategy that they are implementing to increase interest in participation in rugby globally, to grow the game in places that have such contested histories with the sport, there is a need to at least *try* something different.

The emphasis on *try* here is to focus on a newer and different version of the game. Difference is key, and a different version of the game, such as sevens, has shown growth potential and may appeal to some with an athletics background. Therefore, Africa can take the sevens version of the game and (literally) run with it, and the yearly continental competition and African teams competing in international sevens competition gives the sport momentum. Rugby has seen an increase in popularity in the past decade across Africa, but there are still issues linked to the sport and its association with colonialism, segregation and racism (see Cleophas, 2018). But much of this can arguably be linked to the 15-a-side version of the game, referring back to work referenced earlier in this chapter (e.g. Chappell, 2008; Crawford, 1999; Novak, 2012). The other potential is to increase participation in the women's game as well. A step in the right direction is having a dedicated month (May) to promote the sport and they are taking steps in Africa to create a new awareness of the game (CNBCAfrica, 2018). Both sevens and the women's game are attempts to change perceptions and imaginations of the sport. Because if a team needs to score a *try* to win a match, then the take-away point here is the need to *try* something different. There is a need to get people to try and see beyond negative associations of the past – so to move away from more of the same.

References

Alegi, P. (2010). *African soccerscapes: How a continent changed the world's game*. Athens: Ohio University Press.

Allen, D. (2014). 'Mother of the nation': Rugby, nationalism and the role of women in South Africa's Afrikaner society. *Sport in Society*, 17(4), 466–478.

Bale, J. (2003). *Sports geography*. London: Routledge.

Bale, J., and Sang, J. (1996). *Kenyan running: Movement culture, geography and global change*. London: Frank Cass.

Black, D. R., and Nauright, J. (1988). *Rugby and the South African nation: Sport, cultures, politics, and power in the old and new South Africas*. Manchester: Manchester University Press.

Bolsmann, C. (2011). Thoughts on the first African World Cup: Football, representation and exclusion. *Journal des Anthropologues*, 124/125, 359–371.

Bull, A. (2018). Siya Kolisi, captain and symbol of South African rugby's progress. *The Guardian*, Sport, 27 October.

Business Focus Reporter (2018). Africa is among the fastest-growing rugby fan-bases with 32.7M. *Business Focus Reporter*, 6 August. Available at https://businessfocus.co.ug/africa-is-among-the-fastest-growing-rugby-fan-bases-with-32-7m/

Calderisi, R. (2006). *The trouble with Africa: Why foreign aid isn't working*. New Haven, CT: Yale University Press.

Chappell, R. (2008). Sport in postcolonial Uganda. *Journal of Sport and Social Issues*, 32(2), 177–198.

Cleophas, F. (2018). South African rugby star shines spotlight on the sport's racist past. *The Conversation*, 27 May. Available at https://theconversation.com/south-african-rugby-star-shines-spotlight-on-the-sports-racist-past-97030

CNBCAfrica (2018). In May, a month dedicated to women's rugby in Africa. Available at www.cnbcafrica.com/apo/2018/04/10/in-may-a-month-dedicated-to-womens-rugby-in-africa/

Cornelisen, S. (2007). 'It's Africa's turn!' The narratives and legitimations surrounding the Moroccan and South African bids for the 2006 and 2010 FIFA finals. *Third World Quarterly*, 25(7), 1293–1309.

Crawford, S. (1999). Nelson Mandela, the number 6 jersey, and the 1995 Rugby World Cup: Sport as a transcendent unifying force, or a transparent illustration of bicultural opportunism. In R. Sands (Ed.) *Anthropology, sport and culture*. London: Bergin & Garvey (pp. 119–135).

Darby, P. (2002). *Africa, football and FIFA: Politics, colonialism and resistance*. London: Routledge.

Grundlingh, M. (2015). Showcasing the springboks: The commercialisation of South African rugby heritage. *South African Review of Sociology*, 46(1), 106–128.

Harris, J., and Wise, N. (2011). Geographies of scale in international rugby union. *Geographical Research*, 49(4), 375–383.

Kwoba, J. (2018). Africa on its way up to dominate rugby sevens and 15s. *Xinhua*, 23 February. Available at www.xinhuanet.com/english/2018-02/23/c_136995031.htm

Nabiswa, C. (2018). Rugby Africa adopts new format for 2019 Gold Cup. *Daily Nation*, Sports, 28 November.

Novak, A. (2012). Sport and racial discrimination in colonial Zimbabwe: A reanalysis. *The International Journal of the History of Sport*, 29(6), 850–867.

Obomate, H. (2016). *Factors affecting strategy implementation in Kenyan rugby: A study of the Kenya rugby union*. Unpublished Thesis, United States International University-Africa (Kenya).

Odendaal, A. (1990). South Africa's black Victorians: Sport, race and class in South Africa before union. In J. A. Mangan (Ed.) *Pleasure, profit, proselytism: British culture and sport at home and abroad, 1750–1914*. London: Frank Cass (pp. 13–28).

Rugby Afrique (2018). Rugby Africa cup. Available at www.rugbyafrique.com/rugby-africa-cup/

Rugby Afrique (2019a). Development. Available at www.rugbyafrique.com/development/

Rugby Afrique (2019b). Women's rugby. Available at www.rugbyafrique.com/womens-rugby/

Sikes, M. (2018). Sport history and historiography. *Oxford Research Encyclopedia of African history*. Available at http://oxfordre.com/africanhistory/abstract/10.1093/acrefore/9780190277734.001.0001/acrefore-9780190277734-e-232

Steenveld, L., and Strelitz, L. (1998). The 1995 Rugby World Cup and the politics of nation-building in South Africa. *Media, Culture & Society*, 20(4), 609–629.

Van Der Merwe, J. (2007). Political analysis of South Africa's hosting of the rugby and cricket World Cups: Lessons for the 2010 Football World Cup and beyond? *Politikon*, 34(1), 67–81.

Wise, N. (2014). Socially constructing contexts and imaginations through filmic simulacra: The case of Invictus. *Global Media Journal: African Edition*, 8(1), 146–155.

Wise, N. (2015). Geographical approaches and the sociology of sport. In R. Giulianotti (Ed.) *Routledge handbook of the sociology of sport*. London: Routledge (pp. 142–152).

Wise, N. (2017). Rugby World Cup: New directions or more of the same? *Sport in Society*, 20(3), 341–354.

9 Rugby towards 2030
John Harris

Looking forward

In his book *Towards 2000*, Raymond Williams (1983) outlines how the strongest forms of placeable bonding are at the local level. Rugby has long been recognised as a sport that can bring people together and foster a sense of identity. The contributors to this collection have all shown how rugby takes on a variety of different forms and that the game remains an activity which can transcend boundaries. While not as significant a date as the start of a new millennium, I use 2030 as a point in time here to question what the future may hold for rugby and consider what changes are likely to happen in the next ten years. This final chapter also brings together a number of the main points made within the preceding chapters and briefly touches upon some key contemporary issues.

We already know that the 2023 Rugby World Cup (RWC) will take place in France, and there is some discussion of bids by both Argentina and the USA to host the 2027 event. If the USA were to host the event, then they will follow Japan and France in a pattern where a RWC competition takes place in a country one year ahead of an Olympic Games. Would this just be a coincidence or point the way towards an emerging pattern in the mega-event landscape? There is, of course, a strong possibility that the event will return to the core in 2027 as both Ireland and Australia have also been linked with hosting the tournament. South Africa may decide to put forward a bid after controversially missing out on hosting the 2023 event. They were the preferred candidate in the evaluation of the RWC board, but in a secret ballot that followed, the council of World Rugby went against this recommendation.

Rugby's stated globalisation may be somewhat exaggerated, but the sport is continuing to develop a wider international profile and reaches to different parts of the world – as clearly outlined in various places throughout this collection. The 2015 RWC attracted record attendances in the stadiums and good television viewing figures. It was also celebrated as being the most economically successful tournament to date generating an economic impact of 2.3 billion pounds (Ernst & Young, 2016). This is important for the money generated by the RWC accounts for a significant percentage of the overall finances used towards the development of the sport across the globe. The competition has changed markedly as the sport has become more commercialised and commodified (see Harris, 2013; Wise, 2017). It is expected that Japan 2019 will also provide a significant financial return and Swart (2017, p. 115) notes that 'the hosting of the event in Japan in 2019 should further add to making the RWC truly global and also lead to more nations hosting this spectacle in the future'.

The elite level of the men's 15-a-side game will continue to be important over the next decade. Yet there are areas here that need to be addressed. The impact of collisions between players as they continue to become bigger and stronger remains a cause for concern. The long-term health of players, given the increased physicality of the game at the elite level, has also come under the spotlight. There will likely be further rule changes to the sport particularly around the breakdown, tackle height and in the scrum. There has been a strong lobby to ban tackling in school rugby (BBC, 2017) and more recent debates about lowering the tackle height following the deaths of three young adult rugby players in France over a period of five months at the end of 2018 (Bull, 2018).

Aside from the numerous issues around player welfare, there will also likely be further changes to make the game more spectator friendly. There is a stated desire by many to have the ball in open play for more minutes in every match and to improve the broader 'spectacle' of the rugby experience. Some traditionalists will balk at the suggestion and fondly look back to an earlier age for where the quality (and character) of a player was only really tested in the mud on a wet Wednesday night in Maesteg. It has often been noted that the complex rules of the sport make it a hard sell to the casual sports fan. In an increasingly competitive environment, where a number of other activities compete for the discretionary time and money that people have, there will continue to be challenges in finding the right balance between tradition and change.

We need to see more innovative and creative strategies to market and promote the game. To take one country as an example, in Scotland, ticket prices for international matches have gone up as the fortunes of the men's national team have improved. At the same time, Edinburgh Rugby continued to play in front of relatively small crowds in the cavernous surrounds of BT Murrayfield and the Scottish Rugby Union attempt to sell tickets for women's Six Nations matches at small venues where most of the seats remained empty. There is a feeling in many places that rugby is an elitist sport and there are nations across the rugby world where females (and males) face significant barriers to participating in the game. Yet there are also a number of individuals and groups striving to take rugby to disadvantaged groups, and the work of organisations such as Play Rugby USA, Beyond Rugby Bermuda and Memphis Inner City Rugby (in just one geographical area as an example) brings rugby to people who would not have had such opportunities in past. Before looking at the importance of rugby (re)gaining recognition as an Olympic sport, I will now briefly consider some of the key places on the periphery that have not been the focus of chapters in this book.

Challenging the European core and developing a world game

As discussions of Brexit dominated the wider landscape of European politics in 2019, European rugby at the elite level continued to remain the preserve of a very small group. Romania challenged this hegemony in the 1980s and yet failed to secure a place to join the Five Nations championship. There was little appetite from the blazers controlling the game to bring Romania into the fold and the revolution of 1989 brought about significant change in the country. The two dominant Bucharest teams that represented the army and the police lost the funding they had received from the state. The open professionalisation of the sport in 1995 also had a major impact as some Romanian players moved away from the country.

Extending an invitation for Italy to join the Five Nations meant that since 2000 a Six Nations competition is now been the premier annual tournament for European international rugby. Clearly, for those who were part of the decision-making process, a long weekend in Milan or Rome was a tempting prospect and something that undoubtedly worked in Italy's favour. Yet since being admitted into this tournament, Italy have often struggled to be competitive, and at the end of the 2019 Six Nations have gone 22 matches without a win in the tournament. At the same time, Georgia have made significant strides forward, and there are occasional representations made discussing the possibility of introducing promotion and relegation from the Six

Nations championship as it is felt that Georgia would be more competitive than Italy at this time. At the end of 2018, and again in early 2019, key stakeholders met to discuss plans for a World League in rugby.

The Rugby Europe championship was won by Georgia in 2017–2018 and Romania took the title the year before that. Prior to this, the European Nations Cup had been the property of Georgia for six consecutive years between 2011 and 2016. Romania were the nearest challengers to Georgia over the past decade and also qualified for the 2019 RWC. However, it was found that one of the players who was part of this qualification campaign, Sione Faka'osilea, had previously represented the Tonga sevens team in 2013, so this made him ineligible to represent Romania. Romania were subsequently disqualified from taking part in the 2019 RWC and were replaced by Russia. Russia, like many other peripheral rugby nations, have a coaching team comprising of a number of individuals from the core rugby nations.

There has already been much good work on rugby in the Pacific Islands (see Dewey, 2008). When original proposals of a World League were first muted, there was some speculation that many of these island nations would even boycott the 2019 World Cup with the proposal being forward described as something that would be 'the death of Pacific Island rugby' (Cully, 2019). The addition of economic powerhouses Japan and the USA to the Four Nations currently competing in the Southern Hemisphere competition was clearly the path that made most sense from a financial perspective. Small islands with tiny populations and poorer economies were never going to be central to any development irrespective of how good the teams could perform on the field. Yet we can only hope that these nations are given opportunities to compete in future competitions and that all nations are supported in a fair and equitable way. More recent proposals putting forward the new structure as the Nations Championship seemed to offer a better scenario for some nations, but this also failed to get the required support from the unions (BBC, 2019).

This collection has offered a snapshot of rugby in a variety of different places on the periphery. There are, of course, far more nations that are not featured within our discussion, and this book is in many ways a starting point to encourage further scholarship on rugby outside the core. China will continue to emerge as an important market for rugby and a whole host of other sports. We started this collection by considering the significance of the first-ever RWC in Asia. An Olympic Games will quickly follow the RWC in Tokyo 2020, and Hong Kong, Singapore and Dubai are firmly established as key locations on the sevens circuit.

The popularity of association football in many nations is often cited as a barrier to the development of rugby. It is important not to position the two sports as oppositional, for many of the best rugby players in the world have also played football. Yet, as discussed in some detail elsewhere, the hegemonic sports culture of any particular nation usually involves an exalted position for a particular code of football which in turn has an impact not only on the other codes of football but also the opportunities for women's involvement in these sports (see Harris, 2010; Markovits and Rensmann, 2010). One of the most significant developments to impact upon the position of rugby in global perspective was the return of the sport to the Olympic Games.

The Olympianisation of rugby

Almost a decade ago, I discussed the Olympianisation of rugby union as something that would be crucial to the development of a more international profile for the sport going forward (see Harris, 2010). This considered some of the challenges that using sevens as a driver for the broader growth of the game would mean and also looked at a scenario where sevens would in time replace the 15-a-side version of the sport as the premier form of rugby. Stewart and Keech (2017, p. 104) argued that 'World Rugby needs to ensure that the Olympic participation in 2016 and 2020 exemplifies the extent to which rugby sevens is a global game'. We can only reflect on the 2016 event at this time, but it is generally agreed that this was a big success with some exciting matches and the first-ever Olympic medal of any kind for Fiji. The particular challenges of developing the game in this nation are captured in the account of Englishman Ben Ryan who was coach of the Fijian team at Rio 2016 (Ryan, 2018). Fiji have long been very popular in sevens rugby for their performances in the annual Hong Kong Sevens tournament and at other international competitions. In Chapter 3, Yoko Kanemasu and Gyozo Molnar highlighted the importance of the sevens game of rugby in this country and the great strides forward made by female rugby players there. While the success of the men's team in 2016 provided a site for national celebration in Fiji, it also brought to an end the unlikely answer to the quiz question as to who were the reigning Olympic champions at rugby. The USA's victory at the Paris Olympics in 1924, when three teams took part in the traditional 15-a-side version of the sport, was the last time that the sport had featured in an Olympiad until 2016. As Lindsey Gatson and Lara Killick have shown in Chapter 4, there is a strong support for rugby in the USA, but there are also significant challenges in developing a professional league in

15-a-side rugby. The USA men's and women's sevens teams have performed well in the World Sevens Series and so could represent a potential medal hope for Team USA in the 2020 Olympic Games. In the early part of 2019, the USA men's team were ranked as the joint best team in the world (with New Zealand) in the World Sevens rankings.

As touched upon in various places within this collection, the shorter sevens version of the sport offers opportunities for nations that would struggle to be competitive in the 15-a-side version of rugby. In a world where we are increasingly presented with modified and bite-sized versions of activities to accommodate what are presented as busy time-squeezed lives, sevens is often positioned alongside the example of Twenty20 cricket as a pointer for the future direction of travel for sport. The 15-man game was used in the earlier Olympic events described above, but sevens as an Olympic sport now also offers opportunities for women's teams and far more potential for some non-traditional rugby nations to be competitive at the elite level. In 2016, the first-ever Olympic title in women's rugby was won by Australia who defeated local rivals New Zealand in the final. A bronze medal for Canada points to the competitive performances of nations beyond the traditional rugby core. The success of Canada and the USA in some of the World Rugby Sevens Series tournaments is important to note here. While not the only factor, the Olympic status of rugby has been very important to the growth of women's rugby in a variety of different nations. In developing the case for inclusion at the Olympic Games, the IRB needed to put forward a sport that would be played by both men and women. This then was central to the success of the bid, and there is now an even stronger sense that rugby is a sport for both sexes.

World Rugby (2017) have outlined their ambition for developing this area:

> By 2025, rugby will be a global leader in sport, where women involved in rugby have equity on and off the field, are reflected in all strategy, plans and structures, making highly valued contributions to participation, performance, leadership and investment in the global game of rugby.

Dee Bradbury of Scotland became the first woman to be appointed president of a major rugby nation in 2018. Women's rugby was first played at the Commonwealth Games in the Gold Coast, Australia in 2018 (20 years after the introduction of men's rugby into the event at Kuala Lumpur) with New Zealand winning both of these inaugural competitions. There are, of course, still many challenges impacting upon the development of women's rugby as highlighted in the chapter on the Fijiana by Yoko Kanemasu and Gyozo Molnar. In Chapter 8, Nicholas Wise also touched upon some of these in looking at the positioning of rugby across a number of African nations where profound gender inequalities impact upon the opportunities for women to play the sport. Before moving on to the concluding part of this chapter, I will now turn to a short discussion of labour migration as another important topic impacting upon core-periphery relations over the next decade.

Labour migration

As noted earlier, there was tightening of the rules regarding the residency requirements that will come into effect at the end of 2020. As Nicholas Wise and I touched upon in Chapter 2 on Argentina, the influential role of the former Argentina captain and scrum-half Augustin Pichot is very important to note here. As Vice Chairman of World Rugby, Pichot has been an outspoken critic of a system that clearly tilts the balance of power even further towards the core. Yet it should also be noted here that much of the migration of elite players is largely within the core. In the Scotland squad for the 2015 RWC, 12 of the 31 players who made up the squad were born outside of Scotland but only one of these (Tim Visser) was from a country (Netherlands) outside of the core (Cullen and Harris, 2019). Many of these Scotland players, as was also the case with players representing a number of other nations at England 2015, qualified for the country they were representing via rule 8b of the World Rugby regulations whereby they had a parent or grandparent born in that country. As Mike Rayner shows in Chapter 6 on Cyprus, and Danyel Reiche and Axel Maugendre demonstrate in their work on Lebanon in Chapter 5, there are many people who enjoy opportunities to play international rugby having qualified via ancestry. The high-profile professional players get all the attention here, but international rugby is also replete with stories of players who love the game getting opportunities that they would not have had in the nations they were born in. There are many human-interest stories of athletes playing on the periphery that we should not overlook.

A more recent and contentious issue concerns the eligibility of players who qualify for a nation via residency rules (rule 8c of the World Rugby regulations). As a professional sport, and as a business, rugby players are no different to other skilled workers who can capitalise on the skills they have to earn a decent living. This has resulted in something of a 'brawn drain' for a nation such as Tonga where opportunities presented in other nations are life-changing ones for players and their families. The targeted recruitment of athletes to represent national teams and the identification and tracking of so-called project players continues to be a topic of much debate. An article in the *Scotsman* (November 15, 2015) reflecting on the 2015 RWC captured this well:

> We have just had a cracking World Cup, the best perhaps, although I still have a fondness for the 1995 edition, but am I alone in thinking that the sight of South Africans, New Zealanders and various itinerant islanders, especially Fijian wingers, flying flags of convenience undermines the integrity of international rugby and leaves a bad taste in the mouth?

More needs to be done to provide coaching opportunities for coaches from outside of the core nations. As in many other sports, this is not simply a case of putting on coaching courses, and celebrating a rhetoric around inclusivity and sport for development initiatives, but by providing real and tangible opportunities to those from the periphery to coach at the elite level of the game. Rugby in many parts of the world, to borrow from a phrase used to describe the universal simplicity of football, is often played in an environment of 'jumpers for goalposts'. This is the base and the very heart of sport that is played for fun, with limited resources, and a focus on play. In Chapter 7, Gareth Hall and Arianne Reis show how many children in Brazil have been introduced to rugby through programmes that focus on using sport as a means of bringing about social change. Many of the contributors to this collection have shared insights from their fieldwork and clearly highlighted the importance of understanding the particular local context. There is no 'one size fits all' model that can be used here when we look at rugby for development.

The final whistle

A number of different topics have been explored in this collection. We have looked at some of the key issues facing the sport in a macro perspective and also the specific challenges within particular locales. Sevens will remain a part of the Olympic Games up until at least 2028 and the future of any sport is clearly enhanced by having Olympic status. The funding that is then afforded to Olympic sports in some nations is clearly good for the game and the fact that this is something provided for both women and men is crucially important to the future development of the sport in a broader perspective. Many of the contributors to this collection have clearly shown how this has impacted upon the sport in a range of different locales. The associated funding that comes with Olympic status in many nations outside the core means that rugby now has a legitimacy that it may not have had in the past. A HSBC (2016) report into the future of rugby looked forward ten years to a time where participation numbers have doubled and countries with little rugby tradition will be internationally competitive in sevens competitions.

The car bumper stickers and postcards that stated *Give Blood: Play Rugby* or *Rugby Is a Sport for Men with Odd-shaped Balls* may be less visible today. These both reflect back to a time where the sport was often positioned as something that took place in a hyper-masculine environment based around violence on the pitch and the excessive consumption of alcohol off it. This may not have totally disappeared, and any transgressions of rugby players are seized upon by sections of the media as evidencing the fact that rugby may still be considered to be a game for hooligans (see Richards, 2007). Yet in many cases, significant progress has been made, and rugby is increasingly viewed as a game for both males and females.

Considerable inequalities between nations have limited the development of the sport in a global perspective, and much of this has been based upon a reluctance by the core to give up any control (see Harris, 2010; Harris and Wise, 2011). The United Nations Sustainable Development Goals (SDGs) can be used as a driver here for the sport to clearly engage with key issues and bring about significant social change (United Nations General Assembly, 2015). Rugby can make a contribution to a number of the SDGs such as ensuring healthy lives and promoting well-being for all (SDG 3), ensuring inclusive and quality education for all (SDG 4) and achieving gender equality and empowering all women and girls (SDG 5). As many of the contributors to this book have clearly shown, such work is well underway in a variety of different places across the world where rugby is being used as a force for good. Rugby has often been recognised as a sport with a strong social conscience based around the core values of integrity, passion, solidarity, discipline and respect. These were the character-building characteristics of rugby identified by World Rugby member nations in 2009.

Rugby union is clearly at a crucial stage in its development as an international sport. In discussing broader social change, Williams (1983) wrote about a 'journey of hope'. This wording seems appropriate as a phrase to be used in encouraging key stakeholders to work towards a more progressive and inclusive future for rugby union. We can then embark on a journey where there is a degree of uncertainty about who the semi-finalists will be for the 2027 RWC. We may also look forward to a time where a team from outside of the hegemonic core claims the Women's RWC in 2025. Nations on the periphery should be provided with opportunities to host major rugby events by the end of the decade. The challenges around player eligibility and migration will continue to present some challenges in an increasingly globalised world. Sevens could be firmly established as one of the highlights of the Olympic programme and coaches from Tier 2 and Tier 3 rugby nations are leading Tier 1 nations into the biggest tournaments. The bounce of a rugby ball is unpredictable, but the next decade could be one of the most important in the whole history of this wonderful game.

References

BBC (2017). Ban tackling in school rugby for safety, experts demand. *BBC News Health*, Available at www.bbc.co.uk/news/health-41386706

BBC (2019) Nations championship: World Rugby abandons plans for new world league. Available at www.bbc.co.uk/sport/rugby-union/48698587

Bull, A. (2018). France facing up to clamour for rugby to change after spate of tragedies. *The Guardian* (online), Available at www.theguardian.com/global/2018/dec/18/france-rugby-union-deaths

Cullen, J., and Harris, J. (2019). Two project players and a kilted kiwi with a granny from Fife: (re)presenting Scotland at the 2015 Rugby World Cup, *Sport in Society* (Online first). Doi: 10.1080/17430437.2018.1555227

Cully, P. (2019). 'The death of Pacific Island rugby': World Rugby blasted over World League. Available at www.stuff.co.nz/sport/rugby/international/110939176/the-death-of-pacific-island-rugby-world-rugby-blasted-over-world-league

Dewey, R. (2008). Pacific islands rugby: Navigating the global professional era. In G. Ryan (Ed.) *The changing face of rugby: The union game and professionalism since 1995*. Newcastle: Cambridge Scholars Publishing (pp. 82–108).

Ernst & Young (2016). *The economic impact of the Rugby World Cup 2015*. London: Ernst & Young.

Harris, J. (2010). *Rugby union and globalization: An odd-shaped world*. Basingstoke: Palgrave Macmillan.

Harris, J. (2013). Definitely maybe: Continuity and change in the Rugby World Cup. *Sport in Society*, 16(7), 853–862.

Harris, J., and Wise, N. (2011). Geographies of scale in international rugby union. *Geographical Research*, 49(4), 475–483.

HSBC (2016). *The future of rugby: An HSBC report*. London: HSBC Holdings.

Markovits, A., and Rensmann, L. (2010). *Gaming the world: How sports are reshaping global politics and culture*. Princeton, NJ: Princeton University Press.

Richards, H. (2007). *A game for hooligans: The history of rugby union.* Edinburgh: Mainstream.
Ryan, B., with T. Fordyce (2018). *Sevens heaven: The beautiful chaos of Fiji's Olympic dream.* London: Orion.
Stewart, J., and Keech, M. (2017). The globalization of rugby sevens: From novelty to the Olympic Games. In J. Nauright and T. Collins (Eds.) *The rugby world in the professional era.* London: Routledge (pp. 93–107).
Swart, K. (2017). The Rugby World Cup as a global mega-event. In J. Nauright and T. Collins (Eds.) *The rugby world in the professional era.* London: Routledge (pp. 108–117).
United Nations General Assembly (2015). Transforming our world: The 2030 agenda for sustainable development. Available at www.un.org/sustainable development/summit/#overview
Williams, R. (1983). *Towards 2000.* London: Chatto & Windus.
Wise, N. (2017). Rugby World Cup: New directions or more of the same? *Sport in Society*, 20(3), 341–354.
World Rugby (2017). Accelerating the global development of women in rugby 2017–2025. Available at https://pulse-static-files.s3.amazonaws.com/worldrugby/document/2017/11/23/1c969b2a-58e7-4172-b81b-da0cdd241dec/World-Rugby-Womens-Rugby-Development-plan-2017-2025.pdf

Index

Aouad, Sarah 51, 53
Algeria 91, 96–7
Argentina 2, 7, 12–22, 37, 55, 78, 80, 91, 104, 110
Asian Games 57, 61, 62
Australia 1, 5–6, 9, 12–13, 18–19, 27, 61, 68–9, 104, 109
Azerbaijan 71

Bai, Seremaia 29, 35
Baker, Perry 41
basketball 42, 44, 55, 82
Baudino, Enzo 50, 54–5
Berro, Mohammad 51–2
Beyond Rugby Bermuda 106
Binikos, Andrew 74
Botswana 93, 95, 97, 100
Bradbury, Dee 109
Brazil 8, 14, 17–18, 22, 77–87, 91, 111
British Empire 13, 65, 68
Brexit 106

Cameroon 91, 97
Canada 6, 38–9, 44, 96, 109
Carter, Dan 4
Cheika, Michael 50
Chile 14, 17–18
China 91, 107
colonial 24–5, 67, 78, 90; colonialism 64, 90, 101; postcolonial 25, 28, 93
Commonwealth Games 109
Creevy, Augusten 19
cricket 13, 65, 67, 78–9, 90, 94, 109
Cyprus 8, 53, 64–75, 110

Diallo, Amady 53
Dubai 107

England 1, 2, 4–6, 12–13, 20, 32, 40, 44–6, 51, 53, 56, 60–1, 67, 72, 83, 110
entertainment 69, 79

Faka'osilea, Sione 107
Fiji 7, 24–35, 108, 110
Fijian soldiers 52
Five Nations 106
Foden, Ben 44
Football World Cup 4, 13–14, 91
foundation nations 1, 20, 90
France 1, 3, 13, 20, 40, 52–3, 55, 60–61, 104–5

Galindo, Manuel 18
gender issues 3, 25–6, 30–1, 35, 39, 80–1, 110, 112
Georgia 9, 72, 92, 106–7
Germany 4, 96
Ghana 91, 97, 100
globalisation 2–4, 8, 17, 71–2, 104
Greece 65, 71

hegemonic sports culture 108
Hong Kong 25, 38, 30–1, 33–4, 96
Hong Kong Sevens 6, 107–8

inclusive 75, 83, 87, 96, 112
International Rugby Board (IRB) 15, 30, 79, 109
Ireland 1, 6, 41, 52, 104

Irish soldiers 52
Isles, Carlin 41
Italy 2, 9, 17, 41, 106–7
Ivory Coast 91–3, 97–8, 100

Jammal, Abdallah Ali 50–2, 58
Japan 1, 3–6, 9, 16, 19–20, 28, 30–1, 33, 92, 101, 104–5, 107
journey of hope 9, 112

Kazandjian, Danny 57
Keeler, Paul 43
Kenya 92, 96–100
Knio, Douha 51, 59

Lebanon 8, 50–62, 110
Lewis, Steve 43

Madagascar 97, 100
Major League Rugby (MLR) 42, 44–5
Mandela, Nelson 94
Makarios, Archbishop 65
masculine 22, 26, 29, 46, 82, 112
Mauritius 97, 100
mega-events 3–4, 14, 35, 85, 91, 104
Memphis Inner City Rugby 106
migration 44, 110, 113
Monaco 71
Morocco 91, 96–8, 100

Namibia 92–3, 96–100
Netherlands 110
New Zealand 1, 3, 4–6, 12–13, 18–19, 30, 32, 38, 41, 69, 109
Nigeria 91, 97, 100

Olympic Games 6, 10, 14, 47, 58, 61–2, 110; Paris (1924) 38, 108; Tokyo (1964) 4; Los Angeles (1984) 4; Rio (2016) 7, 21–2, 27–9, 40–1, 57, 74, 78–80, 83, 85, 87, 98, 110; Tokyo (2020) 4, 109; Paris (2024) 4

Pacific Islands 27, 31, 107
Peters, Greg 17
Pichot, Augustin 7, 15, 18–21, 110
player eligibility 60–1, 72, 107, 110–11, 113
player welfare 21, 45, 82, 105
Play Rugby USA 106

Premiership Rugby 46, 83–5
PRO Rugby 43–5

Ramadan, Mazen 51, 58
Romania 106–7
Rugby Afrique 93–100
Rugby Championship 7, 12, 15, 17–18, 21, 74, 96
Rugby League 8, 50–1, 55–8, 60–2
Rugby World Cup (RWC) 1–9, 14, 16–17, 20, 32, 70, 73, 91–3, 96, 98, 101, 104–5, 107, 110–11, 113; RWC tournament results (1987–2015) 12–13
Russia 6, 22, 91, 107
Ryan, Ben 108

Samoa 6
SANZAR 17–21
SANZAAR 19–21
Schoninger, Doug 43–4
Scotland 1, 6, 13, 37, 41, 93, 105, 109–10
Senegal 55, 97, 100
Singapore 107
Six Nations 74, 96, 106
Slovakia 71
South Africa 1, 5, 8, 12–14, 18–19, 69, 90–4, 96, 98–100, 104
spectators 3, 26, 29, 33–4, 38, 41, 71, 105
Sport-for-Development (SfD) 77–87
Suleiman, Michel 58
Super League 42–3
Super Rugby 7, 12, 15, 18–21, 74

tackle 46, 105
television 5, 9, 20, 27, 41, 55, 64, 70, 105
Tonga 107, 110
Tri-Nations 15, 18
Try Rugby 77–8, 83–7
Tunisia 96–100
Turkey 65

Uganda 93, 96–100
United Nations Sustainable Development Goals 112
United States of America (USA) 5–6, 8–9, 37–46, 52, 55, 60, 84, 104, 106–9
Uruguay 14, 17–18

Visser, Tim 110
voting 17, 20, 55

Wales 1, 4, 6, 9, 13, 90
Williams, Raymond 9, 104, 112
Williams, Shane 4
Wills, Tom 67–8
Women's Rugby World Cup 7, 25–8, 33–5
World Rugby (WR) 2, 4, 6–8, 15, 17, 19, 21, 30, 43, 59, 61–2, 73–5, 79, 83–4, 86, 93–5, 98, 104, 108–10;
WR participation figures 4, 14, 27, 31, 80
world systems theory 17
Wrigglesworth, Steve 51, 53, 59
Wyles, Chris 43

Youth Olympics 21

Zambia 97, 100
Zimbabwe 92–3, 96–100

For Product Safety Concerns and Information please contact our EU representative GPSR@taylorandfrancis.com
Taylor & Francis Verlag GmbH, Kaufingerstraße 24, 80331 München, Germany

www.ingramcontent.com/pod-product-compliance
Lightning Source LLC
Chambersburg PA
CBHW070739230426
43669CB00014B/2507